Neil H. Jacoby
University of California
Los Angeles

James E. Howell
Stanford University

EUROPEAN ECONOMICS— EAST AND WEST

Convergence of Five European Countries and the United States

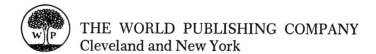
THE WORLD PUBLISHING COMPANY
Cleveland and New York

Published by THE WORLD PUBLISHING COMPANY
2231 West 110th Street, Cleveland, Ohio 44102

Published simultaneously in Canada by
Nelson, Foster & Scott Ltd.

Library of Congress Catalog Card Number: 67–19292

PRINTED IN THE UNITED STATES OF AMERICA

First Printing

To Clair and Penny

This book is part of

The World Series in Economics

E. E. *Liebhafsky,* Consulting Editor

Monographs:

THE CLASSICAL THEORY OF ECONOMIC POLICY
  Warren J. Samuels

TECHNOLOGY, MANPOWER,
  AND RETIREMENT POLICY
  Edited by Juanita Kreps

ECONOMIC DEVELOPMENT IN ACTION:
Theories, Problems, and Procedures as Applied
  in the Middle East
  Taghi T. Kermani

THE DEMAND FOR MONEY
  William J. Frazer, Jr.

PROFESSIONAL POWER AND AMERICAN MEDICINE:
  The Economics of the American Medical Association
  Elton Rayack

INVESTMENT BANKING AND THE
  NEW ISSUES MARKET
  Irwin Friend, James R. Longstreet, Morris Mendelson,
  Ervin Miller, and Arleigh P. Hess, Jr.

Readings:

READINGS IN MICROECONOMICS
  Edited by David R. Kamerschen

AUTHORS' PREFACE

This book is a series of essays on salient economic trends in five major European economies, east and west of the Iron Curtain, and on the meaning of these trends for Americans. The United Kingdom, France, the Federal Republic of Germany, Poland, and the Soviet Union are examined. The focus of attention is upon emerging problems of economic policy and upon the methods being used by governments to improve systems of economic guidance. Changes in the nature of governmental and enterprise management in order to attain national economic goals are our central concern.

We have sought in these essays to convey a general knowledge of the contemporary status of the five economies, to offer insights into their future movements, and to point to lessons of value to the United States. The essays are brief, general, impressionistic, and speculative. We have compared and synthesized economic trends and policies in the five countries, as described by specialists in each and in the light of our discussions with some of their leaders, and have drawn inferences useful to Americans. We have not sought to write a comprehensive textbook on comparative economic systems, nor do we present this book as a systematic treatment of comparative economic policy. Directing it to the general reader as well as to the scholar, we have omitted charts and footnotes. Nevertheless, we have taken pains to verify the facts upon which our observations are based. Appended to each chapter is a selected list of readings to aid those readers who wish to pursue its subject further.

As economists on the faculties of the Graduate Schools of Business at the University of California, Los Angeles, and at Stanford University, we have long had a professional concern with the management of individual enterprises as well as of economies. We have visited the United Kingdom and Western Europe frequently since World War II as educators, as official representatives of the United States Government, or as directors of European business corporations. One or both authors visited Eastern Europe in 1966 and again in early 1967. The basic informational inputs into these essays derive from these studies and experiences.

The direct inspiration for this book, however, came from our participation in the 1966 *Journey for Perspective*. This was a concentrated study-tour of the five European countries by a selected group of graduate students and deans of the five graduate schools of business administration on the Pacific Coast of the United States. *Journey* had the broad purpose of creating an understanding among potential American businessmen of the achievements, problems, and prospects of economic and enterprise management in leading European countries. Thus, they might gain perspectives of their own country and, as executives, enhance their contributions to its development. *Journey* was essentially a traveling seminar. Conferences and interviews were conducted with business, governmental, and academic leaders of the five countries, which afforded the participants an unsurpassed opportunity to learn about problems confronted and how they were dealt with. Our seminars following these meetings produced many of the reflections set down in this book.

We express deep gratitude to William J. Bird, founder and

president of the Journey for Perspective Foundation, for arranging a valuable program in 1966, and to Harry Krusz, our tour director. We are grateful to those Pacific Coast business corporations whose financial support made our journey possible. We thank our fellow academics, Richard Johnson of the University of Washington, Lawrence Vance of the University of California, Berkeley, and Kenneth Trefftz of the University of Southern California, for ideas and information. We are indebted to several readers, including Professor Neil Chamberlin and Dr. Gerhard Colm, for useful comments on the manuscript. Most of all, we thank the many distinguished and burdened gentlemen who took time to meet us and to respond to our questions. A list of their names and affiliations follows. Because our interviews with them were conducted with candor and on a promise of no attribution, we have not ascribed opinions to any of them in this book.

We hope that the student of comparative economic systems and policies, as well as the general reader, will find these essays useful. Although the essays were written by American economists primarily for an American audience, we venture to believe that some of our findings and observations may also be of interest to our European friends. Analysis of contemporary affairs is a perilous exercise at best. We seek our readers' pardon for any inadvertent errors of fact and their toleration for opinions that may differ from their own.

> *Neil H. Jacoby*
> University of California
> Los Angeles
> *James E. Howell*
> Stanford University

April, 1967

PERSONS WHO CONFERRED
WITH PARTICIPANTS IN
JOURNEY FOR PERSPECTIVE

England

Mr. J. Paul Getty, international petroleum executive; Sir Michael Fraser, C.B.E., Deputy Chairman, Conservative Party; Mr. Brian Walden, M.P., Labour Party; Mr. Eldon W. Griffiths, M.P., Conservative Party; Mr. Geoffrey Johnson Smith, M.P., Conservative Party; Mr. Alan Fitch, M.P., Labour Party; Sir Eric Roll, K.C.M.G., C.B., Permanent Under-Secretary of State, Department of Economic Affairs; Lord Boothby of Buchan and Rattray Head, K.B.E.; Professor Benjamin C. Roberts, London School of Economics and Political Science; Professor Harold Rose, London School of Economics and Political Science; Professor Harold Edey, London School of Economics and Political Science; Mr. P. B. A. Moore, C.M.G., Ministry of Defence; Sir Geoffrey Crowther, Chairman, The Economist Newspaper Ltd.

France

Mr. Guy Lhérault, Directeur, École des Hautes Études Commerciales; Mr. Curtis Prendergast, Chief, *Time-Life* News Service, Paris; Mr. Stephen Laird, Editor, *France Actuelle;* Hon. Roger A. Ockrent, Belgian Ambassador to the O.E.C.D.; Mr. Henri Koch, Director of Economic Development, Banque de France; Mr. Duhamel, Economist, Banque de France; Mr. Bernard Cazes, Chef de Cabinet, Commissariat Général du Plan, d'Equipement et de la Productivité; Mr. Jean-Jacques Bonnaud, Chief of Mission, General Commission for National Productivity; Mr. Jean-Claude Servan-Schreiber, Député de Paris, Assemblée Nationale, and Publisher, *Les Echos;* Mr. Vincent Joyce, Public Affairs Counsellor to the U.S. Ambassador, NATO.

U.S.S.R.

Mr. Stanislas M. Menchikov, Deputy Director, Institute of World Economy and International Affairs, U.S.S.R.; Mr. Anatoli I. Shapiro, Economist, Institute of World Economy and International Affairs, U.S.S.R.; Mr. V. Shamberg, Economist, Institute of World Economy and International Affairs, U.S.S.R.; Mr. Vadim Galushko, Director, Institute of Soviet-American Relations, U.S.S.R.; Mr. Ontchishkin, Central Planning Commission, U.S.S.R.; Mr. Zhukov, State Labor Commission, U.S.S.R.; Mr. Katz, Economic Counsellor, U.S. Embassy, Moscow; Mr. Breimen, Political Counsellor, U.S. Embassy, Moscow.

Poland

Professor Tadeusz Lychowski, University of Warsaw and Polish Chamber of Foreign Trade; Professor Rostroyski, University of Warsaw and Polish Chamber of Foreign Trade; Hon. John A. Gronouski, U.S. Ambassador to Poland; Mr. Hartrey, Cultural Attaché, U.S. Embassy, Warsaw.

Germany

Hon. John A. Calhoun, American Minister to Berlin; Mr. Jerome Livingston, Eastern Affairs Section, U.S. Ministry to Berlin; Mr. James Nelson, Economic Section, U.S. Ministry to Berlin; Mr. Brandon Gross, Political Section, U.S. Ministry to Berlin; Hon. Karl König, Senator, City of Berlin; Hon. Edmund H. Kellogg, American Consul General, Düsseldorf; Dr. Herbert Gross, Economist and Journalist, Düsseldorf; Dr. Ernst W. Mommsen, General Director, Thyssen Roehrenwerke, Düsseldorf.

CONTENTS

1. Guidance Systems and Economic Goals

The British economist, Walter Bagehot, wrote that "money does not manage itself." We may paraphrase his famous dictum by saying that "national economies do not manage themselves." Whether they are market-directed, like the U.S. economy, or centrally planned, like the economy of the U.S.S.R., economies can attain optimal performance only through the deliberate intervention of the national government. While the nature and scale of governmental economic management differs radically among countries, some using a loose rein and others directing every detail of economic activity, some kind of governmental guidance system is necessary.

The usual centralized-decentralized or private-state distinction refers to the poles of a continuum rather than to a dichotomy. Although all large industrialized economies are technically "mixed" because they fall between the polar extremes, the mixture varies greatly. Thus, in spite of a few free markets and a little private enterprise in the Soviet Union, and some state enterprise and government-regulated markets in the United States, the differences between these economies justify calling one socialist and the other capitalist.

Common Economic Tasks

All economic systems represent efforts to solve three basic common problems. First of all, there is the problem of deciding how to allocate the limited supply of economic resources—land, labor, capital, management—that are available. In more familiar terms, this is the problem of choosing the product-mix. By and large, capitalist economies solve this problem by permitting privately owned enterprises to compete in open markets for the favor of buyers who are free to spend their disposable income as they wish. Socialist countries, like the Soviet Union, solve the problem by detailed central planning of resource allocation and production schedules, and by rationing consumer goods.

Another problem is that of optimizing the output of goods and services with the resources that are available. In more familiar terms, this is the task of avoiding "waste" as a result of unemployed or inefficiently employed resources. The market-oriented economies of the West try to deal with this problem by maintaining effective competition, and by fiscal and monetary policies that assure a level of aggregate demand for goods and services that will erase unemployment without at the same time creating intolerable price inflation (i.e. a full-employment level of demand). This is an indirect or market-using approach. In communist countries, the state plan controls enterprises, and consumer demand has so far been rationed over the amount of goods and services available.

A third abiding economic problem is that of choosing between present and future consumption. Decisions must be made regarding the relative amounts of consumption and investment, thus determining the rate of capital accumulation and growth. Again, market-oriented economies leave this decision to the individual recipients of income, who decide how much to save and how much to spend on consumer goods. Part of the problem is also placed in the hands of the legislative bodies of governments, which decide how heavy shall be the tax burden and what will be the composition of government expenditures. By contrast, in a centralized economy the decision about present versus future consumption is made at the highest level of government, and then transmitted downwards to individual resource managers as compulsory plans. If the preferences of consumers are given any weight, it is because of their roles as political constituents. It is here more than anywhere else that centrally directed and market-oriented economies differ in practice.

The term "guidance system" has come into common usage in the Space Age. It is the mechanism whereby a complex electronic system adjusts to changes in internal or external conditions, and is intended to keep the system (an aircraft, missile or space vehicle, for example) moving toward an assigned target. We can fruitfully conceive of economic guidance systems utilized by governments to keep national economies moving toward the economic goals of full employment, price-level stability, maximum growth, and external balance. An economic guidance system may be partly automatic, with "built-in" adjustment factors, and partly discretionary, with deliberate adjustments made by the economic decision-makers. The focal point of attention in this book is upon the way in which the economic guidance systems of market-oriented and centrally-planned economies are working today, upon the defects and problems that have arisen under various systems, and upon the probable nature of changes in them.

Three Hypotheses

Three hypotheses emerge from our examination. The first and more fundamental one is that *optimum performance by advanced economies requires a judicious and possibly changing blend of central economic management and decentralized competitive market direction.* As the socialist economies of Eastern Europe, highly centralized since World War II, have recovered from the war and grown, the defects of centralized direction have become obvious. Each of these countries is now finding it *economically* necessary to rely more heavily on the guidance of competitive market pricing and profits.

At the other extreme, the essentially capitalist economies of the United States and Western Europe, which have long enjoyed the enormous advantages of the competitive market as an economic guide, have found that this guidance system has its limitations in dealing with medium- and long-term problems. They are finding it desirable to introduce a measure of central planning in order to maintain satisfactory progress toward national goals.

All of this leads to the second thread that runs through this book: *the increasing appearance of convergence among the systems of economic management of advanced countries*. Both Western and Eastern economies confront difficult tasks in making adjustments. However, the socialist economies confront a larger problem in incorporating competitive market guidance into their economic systems than do the Western economies in adding elements of state central planning to their systems. Incorporating a substantial degree of market guidance into a centralized society is bound to require more basic changes, and to have greater political and social repercussions, than adding elements of central planning to a market economy. The Soviet Union, in particular, is unlikely to resolve its current difficulties in less than a decade. This fact, combined with a slower expansion of its labor force as a result of the "baby gap" during World War II, is likely to make the growth rate of its national product much less than it was during the early fifties.

Meanwhile, the new elements of governmental planning evolved by the Western countries should improve their performance during the next decade. They now realize that there is a proper role for central planning in the operation of a vigorous competitive-market economy. Americans first accepted this fact when Congress passed the Employment Act of 1946. The British have accepted this principle more recently, and the West Germans are likely to follow. France, of course, has since World War II practiced "indicative" four-year or five-year planning of its economy. In the United States we see emerging five-year advance program planning and budgeting in the agencies of the federal government, and increasing rationalization of public expenditure plans of our state and local governments. The concept of a "full employment" federal budget as a condition of economic progress has already gained general acceptance.

The third hypothesis of these essays is that *the economic growth rates of the leading economies will continue to converge during the decade 1966–1975*. The growth of the British and

American economies is likely to be higher than during the past decade, whereas the reverse will hold for European economies, both west and east of the Iron Curtain. While the reasons for these changes differ from country to country, the changes themselves hold important implications. These implications are favorable for the United States, whose balance of international payments should improve. The U.S. dollar should recover its former strength as a key currency in the world. Convergence of growth rates should also create an environment more conducive to political accommodation of West and East.

Implications of Convergence

If our three hypotheses are correct, Americans are unlikely to hear serious boasts by Soviet leaders of "overtaking and surpassing" the United States, or of "burying capitalism." However, Americans would be foolish to interpret impending developments as a justification for complacency. We need to improve our concepts and tools of medium- and long-term economic policy planning. We also need to apply on a wider scale instruments of long-range planning of our physical environment. These challenges must be met without sacrificing economic gains already achieved or compromising our traditional freedoms. They must be met in the face of the continuing and changing fact of Soviet economic power and all that it implies.

2. Britain: A Crisis of Indecision

By the early sixties it was common knowledge that Britain was in trouble. It had become the "sick man of Europe." Its rate of increase in productivity and thus in economic growth had been, by an alarming margin, less than that of any other major Western country: less than 2 per cent as compared with roughly 3 per cent for the whole Atlantic area and the United States, over 4 per cent for the Common Market countries, and even more for France and West Germany. Plagued with recurring balance-of-payments crises—more than a half dozen since 1945—the British economy was regularly being wrenched by "go-stop" monetary actions. The pound limped from one crisis to the next. Twenty years after World War II there was still talk of austerity, of greater sacrifice than ever before. Once the most powerful nation in the world, Britain was humbled by France, which prevented Britain's entry into the European Economic Community (E.E.C.).

What is happening in and to Britain—the home of modern economics, the pre-eminent political model for the whole democratic world, the winner in two world wars, the first modern industrial power? Can or should devaluation of the pound be avoided? What are the prospects for British entry into the E.E.C., and how would its entry affect Britain's economic progress? How can we reconcile economic woes with an undeniably high standard of living, an elaborate system of social security, London's dizzy and youthful vitality as a world center and pacesetter? Surely the loss of an empire and the battering of two world wars are not the whole explanation for the malaise which Anthony Sampson has called Britain's "loss of dynamism."

There has been no lack of diagnosticians. Some emphasize those losses of war and empire, others the high cost in resources and the weak incentives of the welfare state. Still others emphasize an excess (or lack) of central planning, the burden of defense, or the complacency, laziness, and restrictive practices of labor (or management). Everyone talks about prices and costs, wages and profits, inflation and productivity, consumption and saving, investment, exports and imports, the pound and devaluation, and so on.

The visitor returning to Britain in the mid-sixties sensed a new urgency to the talk. He probably came away with the feeling that time really is running out for the British economy. Although one can be encouraged by the apparent weakening of the grip of doctrinaire philosophies and thinking within both major political parties, this is more than offset by the oft-heard British remark that "we will muddle through this time just as we've always done." Britain's friends hope that this optimism is justified, but it is not yet clear that it is.

Background

By the late nineteenth century Britain stood as the world's first and greatest industrial power, dominant in world trade and international finance, head of a mighty empire. To be sure, other countries, especially the United States, were rapidly closing the industrial gap. But, for the moment at least, Britain was supreme.

A half century later, in 1945, after two crushing wars and a major depression during the interwar period, Britain was barely recognizable as the same country. Archaic economic structures and attitudes cast a long shadow over the prospects for recovery. British industry, once vigorous and competitive, was now highly restrictive. The loss of competitive advantage in world markets, practically unnoticed before World War I, reached a climax during the interwar period, when British management turned from competition to restriction—high tariffs, cartelization and other monopolistic arrangements, resale price maintenance, and so on. The result was the protection of inefficiency, the disappearance of innovation, and the sapping of whatever natural vitality remained in British industry.

This industrial turning inward was matched or exceeded by the restrictionist attitudes of a powerful trade-union movement. Scarred by the unemployment and terrible economic insecurity of the twenties and early thirties, trade unionists entered the postwar period as ardently restrictionist as their industrial counterparts. They differed on some things—for example, labor's determination to reduce or abolish economic inequality—but in turning inward, away from competition and innovation, they were agreed. With this "loss of dynamism" there was little chance for a vigorous approach to the plethora of problems that have faced the country in the postwar years: reconciliation to loss of the empire, reconstruction of industrial capacity and housing lost during the war, adjustment to the loss of earnings on overseas investment and the concomitant impairment of ability to import, development of new industries that could compete successfully in world markets, or meeting the mountain of demand deferred for nearly fifteen years.

The Welfare State and Full Employment

The Labour Party came to power in 1945 with a parliamentary majority dedicated to imposing a doctrinaire Fabian welfare socialism on what was a static, prostrate economy. The insecurities of the thirties made maintenance of full employment the paramount goal. The method of achieving it was to apply the newly forged economic ideas of J. M. Keynes. The same insecurities, plus a passionate desire to reduce the rather large degree of income inequality, resulted in what came to be called the welfare state. This was a fairly comprehensive program of health, unemployment, educational, and family benefits designed to guarantee everyone access to some minimum standard of living—a social minimum. The mechanisms for achieving this were large-scale government spending programs financed mainly by payroll and income taxes.

In addition to changing the product-mix so that more social and fewer private goods would be produced, all in a condition of full employment, the Labour Government nationalized a number of industries—coal and steel, among others. It was hoped that nationalization would make these industries more efficient; but the only tool, aside from the reduction of private power, was the concept of marginal cost pricing.

These main goals were, more or less, achieved. Unemployment in Britain has been kept low, usually below 2 per cent of its labor force as compared with 4 to 6 per cent for the United States. Of course, a number of other Western European countries have done as well. Similarly, the social security programs have been successful if we look at the absolute shift of resources to welfare purposes. Britain spends roughly one-ninth of its GNP on welfare, about twice what the U.S. spends (although we spend more per capita). On the other hand, Britain spends less proportionately than Belgium, West Germany, Sweden, and most other European countries. It should be noted that these successes, whether judged modest or extravagant, were achieved without recourse to much, if any, central planning, as the term is understood in Europe. The Conservatives, in fact, when they came into power in 1951 and accepted and confirmed Labour's employment and welfare policies, specifically rejected governmental planning as a tool of economic guidance.

To cite some degree of success for British policy in the postwar period is not to say that all was well. Success in attaining the goals of full employment and a social minimum was purchased at the price of low productivity and an international deficit. In spite of a lessening of income inequality, especially after adjustment for taxes and welfare expenditures, a substantial inequality of wealth persisted. Without gift or capital-gains taxes, the wealthy had a means of escaping from the heavy income and excise taxes. Nationalization of certain industries also did nothing to improve resource allocation.

Britain's competitive position improved little, if any, over the postwar years, and succeeding governments seemed unable to do anything about it. The root cause, of course, was something that only recently has the British government faced resolutely: *the massively restrictive policies and behavior of both industry and labor that caused Britain's growth in productivity to lag behind that of the rest of the Western world.*

The Conservatives' postwar policy was largely "me-tooism." Their thirteen years (1951–1964) of political leadership, as against Labour's six years (1945–1951), puts a heavy responsibility on them for Britain's being Europe's "sick man" twenty years after World War II. They put as little real effort into restoring dynamism to the British economy as did the postwar Labour Government. Everyone's concern seems to have been security and protection. However, some young politicians of both parties have begun to speak forthrightly on these matters in the last few years.

"Go-Stop," Devaluation, and Growth

Determined pursuit of economic security has been costly to the British. Whenever their economy approached full employment, a balance-of-payments crisis forced retrenchment. Private domestic demand, output, and employment were restrained until increased exports and decreased imports relieved the pressure on sterling. As each crisis passed, some precious reserves were lost and the economy's forward momentum was temporarily slowed.

This curse of "go-stop" has been much discussed in and out of Britain. The problem is straightforward. Britain must export a substantial portion of its national product in order to get the imports—foodstuffs and raw materials, especially—it needs to maintain present living standards. But in periods of high employment and prosperity, rising costs put British industry at a competitive disadvantage in world markets. The situation is worsened as domestic prosperity increases already high imports and diverts potential exports (e.g., cars) to protected domestic markets. At this point sterling is threatened, reserves fall, there is talk of devaluation. The next step, if devaluation is to be avoided, is the government's adoption of deflationary "stop" policies—mostly the tightening of credit.

The magnitude of the problem is shown by the fact that there were more than a half-dozen sterling crises in the two postwar decades. Imports are about 14 per cent of Britain's GNP—as compared with 3 per cent for the U.S. and 8 per cent for France. Counting invisibles, this proportion rises to more than 20 per cent. The balance between credits and debits is so close, even in "good" years, that only a 5 per cent rise in commodity and invisible imports puts a severe strain on reserves.

Recurring sterling crises and the correlative "go-stop" policies are, of course, only painful symptoms of Britain's failure to increase productivity so that its goods would be fully competitive in world markets, even during domestic prosperity. This, in turn, is the result of sacrificing long-term growth in favor of high current consumption and security. But now "the future" is here! British economic policy in both Labour and Conservative years was so preoccupied with short-run problems (solving the sterling crisis by deflating and then restoring full employment once the crisis abated) that it is little wonder that Britain fell far behind her Western neighbors, especially France and West Germany.

Planning, British Style

In the immediate postwar years the Labour Government seemed well on the road to a planned, socialist society. Such was not the case. The Labour Government understood neither the concept nor process of planning in a modern industrial state. As we have seen, it focused on short-run objectives to the exclusion of long-run ones, whereas the essence of planning lies in letting long-run goals influence immediate decisions. Although the trade unionists who *were* the Labour Party wanted strong positions in their bilateral bargaining with management, they shared the Conservatives' view that, except in national emergencies, the government should not intervene strongly in economic affairs.

A course of governmental non-intervention is difficult to follow in a modern society where the state necessarily controls the supply of credit, takes through taxes a large part of the national income, directs the allocation of more than a fourth of the country's resources into social uses (welfare, defense, and so on), is charged with using all of its powers to maintain both full employment and balance-of-payments equilibrium, and owns the means of production in a number of key industries. It can be done, of course, as the Conservative governments of the fifties showed. In no mood for planning either a capitalist or socialist society, the Tories simply carried the Labour Government's policies a little further. A cult of antiplanning thus developed in Britain at exactly the time when some of her neighbors were discovering that some government planning was not only compatible with, but actually beneficial to, modern capitalism.

The contrast with France during those years is a strong one. Across the Channel, government was learning to conduct its affairs not by the rule of neutrality but with an eye to encouraging efficiency, productivity, and economic growth. Never as vehemently laissez-faire as the British, the French were comfortable with various amalgams of private and public decisions. Close official relationships between public and private managers were commonplace in France, but nearly unheard of in Britain, where even the government and the managers of the nationalized industries held each other at arm's length.

Then, dramatically, there was a change in Britain. In the early sixties, after a decade in office, the Conservatives evinced a major shift in attitude. Long-range objectives, forecasting, planning, suddenly were the order of the day. Prime Minister Macmillan shook up his Cabinet. New, younger ministers appeared. The venerable Treasury was reorganized to fit the new look. Serious negotiations for Britain's entry into the Common Market were conducted in Brussels. The investment plans of the nationalized industries were more closely co-ordinated with national objectives. A covey of institutional arrangements, of which the National Economic Development Council ("NEDDY") was the most important, emerged to embody the new attitude.

Reasons for this change are not hard to find. First, it was slowly becoming apparent that Keynesian concepts, properly modified, were useful tools for solving long-range as well as short-run problems. Second, the increasing influence of younger people, neither doctrinaire laissez-faire Tories nor nationalization-minded socialists, was beginning to be felt, both in the country at large and within the government. These people were unwilling to continue the sacrifice of long-run economic prosperity to the economic and political gods of the prewar years. They were disturbed by Britain's loss of economic strength in the fifties relative to other Western countries. Finally, talk of economic growth was heard everywhere, including during the U.S. presidential campaign of 1960.

The Brussels negotiations of 1962–1963 may, however, have been the most important factor of all. The British representatives, and all those at home who were involved in the supporting discussions, were forced to think about existing British economic policies, institutions, and goals as never before. They had to analyze and rationalize the British situation in order to compare it with the fast-changing situation within E.E.C. They had to choose between justifying the British methods or else changing them so that Britain could fit into the European pattern. Even though terminated by De Gaulle's "*non*," the Brussels negotiations had a major impact on British thinking. By general election time in 1964 there were definite signs in government circles in London that a "new economic look," born within the Conservative Party, was taking hold. This, of course, was simply the attitude, already prevalent on the Continent, that some long-term central economic guidance is necessary if a predominantly private-enterprise economy is going to grow and prosper as much as its own citizens and its world competitors know is possible.

The Labour Government of Harold Wilson, elected in 1964, understood and accepted this idea. Thus, it is more like the Conservative Government it replaced than the Labour Government of the early postwar period. Differences within the Labour Party, however, and another balance-of-payments crisis early in 1965 generated doubt about how emphatically and vigorously the present Government would be able to embrace raising economic growth as a pre-eminent national objective, and national economic management as a means of achieving it.

Economic Policy Under Labour

Economic policy since the 1964 general elections was totally dominated by the problem of a very large balance-of-payments deficit. From a surplus of £63 million in 1961 the basic balance (current and capital) went to a deficit of £57 million in 1963, and to a tremendous deficit of £769 million in 1964. Booming import demand, lagging exports, and large capital outflows all played a part. Domestically, of course, the economy was in the expansion phase of a cycle, with demand, output, and employment high and rising.

After first gaining some time by negotiating short-term, sterling support loans from the United States and others, conventional steps were taken by the new Government in early 1965 to slow the import and capital drains. The 1964 deficit was thus more than halved in 1965; and it was cut further in 1966. Equilibrium is expected in 1967, thus ending four years of deficits, two of which were of crisis proportions.

Domestically, the deflationary measures of 1965 and 1966 were the familiar ones: higher taxes (purchase and special excises, income surcharges, a Selective Employment tax, and so on), tighter money and credit (larger reserve requirements for banks, hire-purchase controls, higher bank rates), reduced government expenditures (especially of spending on public investment), and a wage-price freeze (to be followed by a period of "severe restraint"). These moves eased expansionary pressures considerably, although unemployment remained low until late 1966, skilled labor and other types of shortages persisted, the money supply was still increasing, and wages and prices continued to rise. Wages, in particular, have failed to stabilize: hourly and weekly earnings in late 1965 were 8 to 10 per cent higher than 1964 levels.

Britain has suffered from over-employment, as the 1.2 per cent unemployment ratio for 1965 shows. One British labor market expert asserted that "full employment" in Britain should be defined as about 97.5 per cent of the work force employed. This ratio would give optimal flexibility to adjustment of the labor force and would promote the growth of productivity. Lord Beveridge, in his celebrated 1945 Report, estimated that full employment would mean 3 per cent unemployment.

The most unusual feature of Labour's economic policy was the Selective Employment Tax of 1966, aimed primarily at shifting labor from service to manufacturing industries. The assumption, of course, was that the latter have a higher marginal productivity and would expand exports. Novel and complex, the tax has aroused a storm of controversy over its eventual impact. Some critics claim it will actually discourage the very things it is meant to stimulate. Yet its deflationary impact, some £315 million in its first year, is unarguable.

In spite of all these efforts, the situation in late 1966 was still serious. Many of Britain's friends could agree with an O.E.C.D. summary which noted that there was "some doubt" that Mr. Wilson's efforts would "bring about the necessary changes in the external balance and in the domestic economy quite as

rapidly as might be desirable." Since then, and partly as a result
of such judgments, the Labour Government has tightened up
even more. The unemployed formed 2.6 per cent of the work
force in January 1967. There can no longer be any doubt of its
determination, despite cries from its trade-union supporters,
that it intends to do whatever is necessary to cool off the domestic
economy and eliminate the payments deficit. Determination will
be necessary, for solution of Britain's short-run problems is proving to be slow and painful.

The National Plan for 1965–1970

We have already discussed Britain's long-run economic problems,
especially the failure of both Conservative and Labour Parties in
the postwar years to advance penetrating, realistic diagnoses
and programs. This, as we have seen, began to change in the
early sixties under Macmillan and change continued under Wilson's Labour Government. One of the initial acts of the Labour
Government was to establish a Department of Economic Affairs.
Its missions are to improve the structure of the British economy,
to balance international payments, and to achieve a satisfactory
rate of growth. A National Plan, issued in September 1965,
attempted to provide a framework for the co-ordination of government policies in the light of certain goals and forecasts for
the remainder of the sixties. Targets and forecasts were set for
the private sector, but these were, in the French style, more indicative than compulsory.

The "forecast-target" rate of increase in GNP to 1970 was 3.8
per cent per annum, higher than the 3.3 per cent of recent years
but certainly low by the standards of other advanced nations. Yet
we cannot accuse Mr. Wilson's government of being unduly cautious, since even 3.8 per cent growth will require a major effort.
As in all European countries, a large part of any growth in GNP
must come directly from improvements in productivity rather
than from a growing labor force. In Britain's case, a 3.8 per
cent growth rate for GNP would require a 3.4 increase in productivity, as compared with the 2 to 2.75 per cent experienced over
the last fifteen years. In a realistic view, the target must be
considered over-optimistic.

How do productivity improvements arise? One way is through
higher capital-labor ratios—that is, through capital investment.

The 1965 plan calls for an annual increase in investment of 5.5 per cent to support the 3.4 per cent change in productivity. A necessary condition of investment, of course, is "non-consumption." So, in Britain's case, as GNP is assumed to rise at a rate of 3.8 per cent in the late sixties, private consumption can be permitted to rise by only 3.2 per cent and public consumption (social goods) by 3.0 per cent. The linkages and leverages are straightforward: average annual percentage increase in investment, 5.5; productivity, 3.4; GNP, 3.8; private consumption, 3.2; public consumption, 3.0. Within the investment aggregate, the leading and strategic item is investment in manufacturing. This has been growing at 2.4 per cent per annum in recent years, whereas the 1965 Plan requires a rate of 7.0 per cent. Investment in electricity, gas and water, and distribution industries will be slowed.

Another route to higher productivity is expansion of investment in human resources. In recent years Britain has increased the percentage of its GNP spent on education. The problem of financing education is much debated. How much education should be user-financed and how much taxpayer-financed? British leaders recognize that advanced education in Britain has been too literate and not sufficiently numerate in purpose, and that more emphasis must be placed upon technological, engineering, and vocational education. The belated development of three graduate schools of business administration reflects this new thinking. However, educational institutions require much time to build and there is a question whether many more years will not pass before the gap has been bridged.

A significant barrier to higher productivity in Britain is unsatisfactory industrial relations. The disastrous seamen's strike of June 1966 demonstrated the necessity of a mechanism like the "cooling-off period" provided in the U.S. Taft-Hartley Act. British management has been neglectful of labor relations, and as a result the union shop stewards, rather than the foremen of the company, function as the shop-floor managers. This means that a worker's rather than a managerial view of performance prevails.

The Plan stressed industrial reorganizations needed to increase efficiency (productivity). It is hoped that private initiative will do the job; but the Government stands ready with encouragement in the form of preferential tax treatment, investment grants, and so on. Similar encouragement will be given to industries which increase overseas sales or help industrialization in less-developed regions within Britain.

The Plan hopes to reduce costs (i.e., raise productivity) by a number of measures encouraging labor mobility (retraining, moving allowances, and so on) and by a vigorous incomes policy designed to hold down wage and price increases. It is hoped— "planned"—that the economy can, as soon as the present short-term difficulties are overcome, expand over the next few years in a balanced fashion, smoothly and steadily, avoiding the "go-stop" tempo of the last twenty years.

Although all of its friends hope that Britain succeeds, they cannot help worrying about the difficult tasks of bringing about major structural changes in industry, ending costly restrictive policies by both labor and management, restraining domestic demand, limiting price and wage increases, and grappling with balance-of-payments problems and the ever-present threat of devaluation. History teaches that structural changes come slowly in a democracy.

Competition and the Market

Lack of vigorous domestic competition is often mentioned as the central cause of the sickness of the British economy. To use McGeorge Bundy's words before the U.S. Senate Foreign Relations Committee in June 1966, Britain "alone among the larger nations of the Atlantic society has so far failed to match her economic efforts to her economic appetites." Perhaps it will take another Dunkirk to stir the people and their political leaders to make the hard adjustments that are necessary to enable Britain to keep pace with the rest of the world. It is easy to be pessimistic about this comparatively prosperous society which is so resistant to change.

Certainly, entering into the Common Market would do much to jar British complacency. There can be no doubt of the pervasive desire of both political parties to enter the Market, largely because they do recognize the salutary effect it would have on the economy. But there are political as well as economic arguments for their positions. A unified Europe will sometime emerge, and Britain's presence in it is necessary to reinforce Western, democratic values. Some Britons see their country as the hinge of unity between Western Europe and the United States. This is exactly the self-image, of course, that makes many Europeans reluctant to admit Britain to the E.E.C. at this time. They argue that Britain must become European, dismissing any thought of a special relation with the United States. A fuller discussion of the problems of enlarging the Common Market is presented at the end of the next chapter.

Thus Britain has to make a number of basic adjustments, political as well as economic, before it can become, as it eventually must, a member of E.E.C. Changes *are* occurring in Britain, but the question is whether they are occurring fast enough. Many observers are skeptical as to whether the British people really will provide sustained support of growth-promoting policies, which inevitably must call for restraints upon consumption and for expansion of private investment. The recent courage of the Labour Government in promulgating unpopular but necessary restrictions and in developing a national economic plan gives Britain's friends reason to hope. They may also be encouraged by the knowledge that Britain's economic growth in the early sixties was somewhat faster than during the previous decade.

Selected Sources and References for Chapter 2

Beckerman and Associates. *The British Economy in 1975.* Cambridge: Cambridge University Press, 1965.

Camps, Miriam. *Britain and the European Community, 1955–1963.* Princeton: Princeton University Press, 1964.

Harrod, Roy. *The British Economy.* New York: McGraw-Hill Book Company, Inc., 1963.

Organization for Economic Cooperation and Development. *Economic Surveys: United Kingdom.* Paris: OECD, July 1966.

Sampson, Anthony. *Anatomy of Britain.* London: Holder and Stoughton, 1962.

Shanks, Michael. *The Stagnant Society.* London: Penguin Books, 1961.

Shonfield, Andrew. *Modern Capitalism.* London: Oxford University Press, 1965.

Theobald, Robert. *Britain in the Sixties.* New York: H. W. Wilson Company, 1961.

3. France: Resurgent Nationalism

A visitor returning to France in the mid-sixties sensed a new mood. It is best described as resurgent nationalism. French political and economic leaders spoke with confidence and self-assurance. They see France resuming her early nineteenth-century role of leadership in a new Europe. The new muscle of the French economy, acquired after fifteen years of rapid growth, plus membership in the nuclear-weapons club, had restored traditional French pride in the motherland. France could offer a third force to the people of Europe, as a counterpoise to the polarity of the Soviet Union and the United States. Europeans no longer should be considered merely as pawns in a struggle between these two superpowers. They must reassert their own identity. Historically, geographically, and even economically, France should be considered the natural leader of the New Europe.

Frenchmen—at least those following the ideas of General de Gaulle—believed that the cold war was over. The probability of conflict in Europe between East and West had become negligible. Americans, they said, need no longer be concerned about the defense of Europe against communist aggression. The time was ripe for relaxing barriers to East-West trade.

French leaders argued that "indicative planning" of her economy afforded a novel and promising form of economic guidance by the government. It combined the best features of socialist central planning with a large measure of market guidance of resources. By generating a voluntary consensus about economic goals and programs among all groups in society, French planning avoided the mandatory features of communist planning. It preserved the essential freedoms of consumers, workers, and private investors.

At the same time, Frenchmen were realistic in their assessment of the economic future. They conceded that the postwar "catching-up" boom was over. No longer could the French economy expand upon a basis of technological modernization, imported labor, and foreign capital. The postwar gains in output, resulting from the application of mass-production and mass-marketing techniques, were behind. Future growth must rely mainly upon new, indigenous forces. France must develop an efficient capital market of its own, the better to mobilize savings and direct them into productive investment. It must dedicate itself to thrusting forward its own scientific and industrial technology, thus reducing the dependency upon the United States.

The new mood in France raised a number of basic questions in the mind of the economic observer. Why had France—like Germany—responded so positively to crises and external pressures whereas Britain had not? Would resurgent French nationalism become so strong as to block the development of the European Economic Community? Would French economic policy— traditionally interventionist and marked by extensive cartelism and government controls—prevent France's full participation in a Europe-wide market? Under what conditions would France cease to oppose the admission of Britain to the Common Market? Precisely how has the new instrument of French planning worked, and did it contribute materially to the growth of the French economy?

Postwar Instabilities

The new mood of France was, in part, a reaction from the sense of humiliation and frustration felt by most Frenchmen during World War II and the years of political instability that followed. Defeated and occupied by Hitler's armies, France was deprived of full partnership in the victory over Nazi Germany and emerged from the war politically divided. It lacked the ego-satisfaction of the British victors. By the same token, it lacked the full stimulus that utter defeat provided the Germans, confronted as they were by the stark necessity of rebuilding a shattered economy.

During the early postwar years, France harbored a large and powerful Communist Party which forced the purge of collaborationist and fascist elements. Bitter dissensions between Communists and the manifold other parties that have traditionally characterized French politics generated extreme political instability. Revolution in Algeria, and the long conflict in Indochina ending in French defeat in 1954 at Dienbienphu, were economically and politically costly. No fewer than eighteen different governments were formed between 1949 and 1958, when the new constitution of De Gaulle inaugurated the Fifth Republic. Political instability was the father of monetary and fiscal instability. The franc was devalued *three* times between 1949 and 1958.

Notwithstanding an unstable political system and the economic inefficiencies produced by persistent price inflation and widespread government controls, France did make economic progress with the help of liberal injections of American economic aid.

Spurred on by Jean Monnet, Director of the General Planning Commissariat, a Four-Year Plan covering the years 1947–1950 was adopted, and later extended to 1952 to match the then-expected duration of Marshall Plan aid. The keynote was modernization of the basic sectors of coal, electricity, steel, cement, agricultural machinery, transportation, fuels, and fertilizers. Although the rates of expansion contemplated for these basic industries under the Monnet Plan were ambitious, the targets for most industries were, in fact, achieved.

The Second Plan, adopted after a gap of one year, covered the period 1954–1957. Unlike the First Plan, which had emphasized reconstruction and renovation of basic industries, the keynote of the Second Plan was comprehensive improvements in productivity and in the quality of industrial production. It was sought to make the French economy, hampered by small-scale family enterprises and traditional techniques, more competitive and efficient. On the whole, the targets of the Second Plan also were achieved. However, their optimistic character required huge investments not matched by the voluntary saving of the people, so that the accelerated expansion of industrial output was purchased at the cost of price inflation and financial imbalance. Shortages of skilled labor led to large wage increases and cost-inflation. Imports burgeoned. The French balance of payments went into deficit. The value of the franc continued to sink.

De Gaulle Returns

The year 1958 marked a turning point in both the political and the economic development of France. General Charles de Gaulle was elected President. Under his leadership, France adopted a new constitution on October 4, 1958, establishing the Fifth Republic and giving the President the strong executive powers characteristic of an American President. It ensured political stability, at least for the time being, and enabled the government to carry out far-reaching reforms touching many aspects of the nation's life. The debilitating war in Algeria was settled by granting the country its independence. The other African colonies of France were also offered their independence, and all except one accepted the offer. French liquidation of its colonial empire was thus expeditiously completed.

Of equal importance were the measures taken by the government of De Gaulle to achieve financial stability and to lay a firm foundation for continued economic growth. The franc was devalued on a realistic basis. A new "heavy" franc was introduced in the ratio of 1 for 10 of the old. Better enforcement of tax laws, combined with control of public expenditures and slower growth of money and credit, finally stopped the endemic inflation that had plagued France for so many years. The Third Plan for

1958–1961 sought to achieve a 4.5 per-cent annual expansion in the national product, within conditions of monetary stability and balanced foreign payments. The economic growth rate was temporarily slowed to about 2.5 per cent a year during 1958 and 1959; but thereafter it again mounted rapidly.

The recently completed Fourth Plan for the period 1962–1965 made a high 5.5 per-cent annual gain in national production the target. Whereas earlier plans had emphasized modernization and industrialization, the Fifth Plan had the broader aims of social as well as economic development. More ample provision was made for housing, education, research and development, transportation and social services, and for industrial progress in some of the laggard regions of France. No reduction was made in hours of work.

The investment program contemplated by the Fourth Plan was again over-ambitious, and led to renewed inflation of wages and prices. The Bank of France restricted money and credit, beginning in the fall of 1963. In September 1963 the Government froze the prices of basic raw materials and reduced the rate of increase in outstanding bank credit. Heavy public spending programs were reduced. As a result of these stern policies, a 6.9 per-cent rise in the price index during 1963 was cut to 2.5 per cent in 1964 and to 2.4 per cent in 1965. While the fast growth of production was reduced somewhat, the value of the franc was maintained near parity, and a comfortable balance-of-payments surplus emerged.

Performance of the Economy

Between 1950 and 1965 France expanded its real national production at an average annual rate of 4.6 per cent. This was an impressive performance, in view of the fact that population grew relatively slowly and the domestic work force grew hardly at all. However, some 900,000 Algerian, Moroccan, Spanish, and Italian workers were added to the labor force. Even so, output *per worker* rose about as fast as in West Germany. Virtually full employment was maintained throughout the period.

France's good economic performance during the past fifteen years may be explained by a combination of factors. That France had been catching up with the large opportunities for technological modernization inherent in an economy that had been laggard before World War II was one reason for rapid postwar growth. Inauguration of national economic planning was another; of this more is said later. Participation in the Common Market and the invigorating effects of competition and market opportunities over a wider area was a third cause. Between the first steps in tariff reduction taken under the Treaty of Rome on January 1, 1959, and the end of 1965, France had eliminated all import quotas and had cut its customs barriers by 70 per cent for E.E.C. countries. Its trade with them climbed over 70 per cent during the seven-year period. A final factor was psychological. The strong drive of French leaders for economic progress derived in part from an effort to erase the humiliation and frustration of wartime occupation and loss of empire, and to restore France to a position of moral and political strength in the world.

At the heart of French economic growth was a rapid rise in productivity. Output per man-hour increased by a yearly average of 4.3 per cent—a rate not exceeded by any other large industrial country in the West. A basic cause was the shift of manpower from low-productivity farms and small shops to high-productivity industries. This remarkable record was also made possible by a rising volume of savings guided toward the financing of investment in private enterprises as well as in public facilities, especially roads, harbors, and education. The tax system was revised to encourage business investment. Value-added taxes were extended, in replacement of old-style turnover taxes, to foster integration and modernization of the industrial structure.

Above all, expectations of economic stability were established by budgetary and fiscal reforms that, by 1965, eliminated an operating deficit from the French national budget for the first time in thirty-five years. Recent French experience teaches the lesson that, at a time of full employment, only when monetary restraint is fortified by fiscal restraint can price increases be kept within tolerable bounds. French economists also found that direct price controls could have only a temporary effect, and were not effective instruments of stabilization over the long term. However, controls of consumer credit were used with good effect. They applied not only to the minimum down-payment and maximum pay-out periods of individual consumer loans, but also to the aggregate amount of loans by consumer credit companies.

Planning—à la française

To what extent, if at all, has "indicative" planning contributed to the growth of the French economy during the past fifteen years? Let us first look at the planning process. As carried on during recent years, a five-year plan begins with a target rate of growth in the GNP agreed upon between the Commissariat Général du Plan and the Treasury. This growth rate is reviewed by the Social and Economic Council, composed of ministers of state and representatives of major economic and academic groups. The Government then adds its targets for balance of payments and "social capital" outlays on housing, urban development, and regional balance.

Various divisions of the Planning Commissariat then prepare detailed production targets for economic sectors and industries that are broadly consistent with the overall target. They work with a series of Commissions whose members are drawn from labor and management organizations in those industries. The Commissions thrash out forecasts of demand, investment requirements, labor requirements, and so on, for their respective industries. Their work is assembled and integrated by the staff of the Planning Commissariat, which makes use of national income accounts, input-output relationships, and econometric models in reconciling industry plans. Tentative industry plans are shuttled back and forth between the Commissions and the Commissariat. Targets for sectors and industries are broken down and built up again by an iterative process to obtain internal consistency for the plan as a whole. When a synthesis has been reached, the draft plan is put before the Government, which submits it to the Social and Economic Council for comment. A debate is then opened before Parliament, followed by final approval of the Government. The entire process of developing a plan from inception to adoption requires two to three years, and officially involves some 4,000 civil servants, business executives, labor leaders, and academicians.

French planning is often called "indicative" as opposed to "imperative" because implementation of plan goals relies mainly upon the voluntary actions of businessmen and other economic decision-makers. However, this is not strictly true. Government utilizes many instruments for carrying out a plan. More than one-third of gross fixed investment in France has been made by public enterprises and governmental departments. National savings flow to a considerable extent through governmentally controlled commercial banks and insurance companies, and the government can and has controlled allocations of credit to the private sector by these institutions. The government also exerts control over private investment activities by licensing their capital issues, as well as by price controls and other direct intervention in the economy. All this is in addition to the *indirect* influence exerted by government upon private spending and investment through its fiscal and monetary policies.

Within these broad constraints, nevertheless, the individual French private enterprise, householder, worker, and consumer retains wide freedom of choice of production, saving, investing, and spending decisions. Governmental controls to implement a French plan are far from complete; and they have been diminishing in recent years, as capital markets have improved and the internal financing capabilities of enterprises have enabled them to act more independently. For these reasons, it is perhaps more accurate to describe French planning as "soft" planning, in contradistinction to the "hard" planning of communist countries where individual enterprise goals are enforced by governmental sanctions.

All serious students of French planning point out the impossibility of *proving* that it has contributed to the growth of the economy. One can never be sure how fast the French economy would have grown without planning. The unplanned economy of Britain grew relatively slowly in the postwar years, whereas the unplanned economy of West Germany grew very rapidly. National economic planning must be evaluated in the context of the particular set of political, social, economic, and historical forces influencing each nation. No single system of economic guidance will be universally optimal.

French planners make only modest claims for the tangible results of planning. They assert that planning has helped to expand the volume of private investment and to direct it into more productive channels by providing an overall growth target to which the government is committed, and by generating information about the expansion of industrial markets implied by this target. Its informational and guidance functions have generated confidence in the private sector and have reduced the amount of error in investment decisions. Some evidence in support of this view is the fact that incremental capital-output ratios in important French industries have been lower than in the corresponding industries of other countries in the Common Market during recent years. It is also pointed out that planning, supplemented by the persuasion of the government-industry consulting machinery and the instruments used by the government, has grouped many inefficient small-scale enterprises into larger and competitively stronger units, thus accelerating changes in the industrial structure of France toward a more efficient configuration. There is also specific evidence to support this contention.

On the other hand, critics of French planning say that overly ambitious growth targets requiring excessively high investment outlays produced serious price inflation, particularly during 1957–1958 and 1962–1963. General price inflation inhibited saving, and the resulting distortions in the price structure led to misdirected investment. The critics also charge that investment funds were allocated in less-than-optimal ways, because the network of governmental controls of capital issues, credit rationing, and selective incentives impaired the workings of a competitive investment market. Finally, they assert that the strength of competitive attitudes and behavior was weakened in some industries as a result of the extensive collaboration of industrial executives in the planning process.

It is impossible to evaluate these criticisms quantitatively or to weigh them collectively against those made by protagonists of planning. Yet certain general conclusions seem tenable on a basis of French experience. *A consensus appears to be emerging that, while national planning has improved France's economic performance, its contribution is limited and planning should not be pushed too far.* Pierre Massé, Chairman of the Commissariat Général du Plan, recently spoke of the Plan as a "general market survey." A senior officer of the Commissariat remarked significantly: "At the least, planning has been an enormously successful exercise in adult economic education!"

National economic planning in a predominantly market-directed economy is likely to hamper economic progress *if its goals are rigid and detailed and are enforced by extensive direct governmental intervention.* The negative effects of planning can be minimized by avoiding precise and rigid goals and direct controls. Instead, plans should be viewed as medium-term market forecasts, subject to revision as unforeseen factors come into play. Goals should be broad and subject to change as a result of exogenous influences, domestic or foreign. Implementation should rely to a maximum extent upon the workings of competitive markets and to a minimum extent upon government intervention. Few will debate the proposition that a national commitment to pursue policies for full employment, a stable price-level, maximum sustainable growth of productivity, and international balance will provide the best possible environment for more stable spending and investment behavior by private firms and households. This, in turn, will improve economic performance by moderating cyclical swings.

It is significant that the Fifth Plan, for the years 1966–1970, set the optimistic goal of a 5 per cent annual gain in GNP, but that it contained provision for annual review and alteration of the Plan as circumstances require. The French Government would be wise to bend strong efforts to making domestic financial and industrial markets more competitive, so that execution of the Fifth Plan can rely more upon market guidance and less upon bureaucratic edicts. France's future economic progress— indeed its ability to participate in and benefit from the Common Market—would be impaired if the traditional tendency toward governmental interventionism should push it in the direction of "hard" planning.

The Technological Gap

French economic leaders express deep concern about the superior technology of the United States, particularly in aircraft, electronics, computers, nuclear applications, and metallurgy. They are worried that the present substantial gap is growing larger. They see the advanced products of American corporations, such as International Business Machines, General Electric, or Litton Industries, taking over increasing shares of European markets. IBM alone occupied about 60 per cent of Western Europe's computer market in 1966. The O.E.C.D. estimated that in 1961 Western Europe had a deficit of $206 million in the two-way flow of payments to and from the United States for licensing, royalties, patents, and other forms of technological knowledge. Some experts believe it may have risen to $1 billion a year by 1966. In addition, there has been a developing "brain drain" of top European scientists and engineers into American employment, either in the United States or in Europe. The French Government resisted the purchase of control of Machines Bull—France's largest computer company—by General Electric in 1965 until it found that only in this way could the company survive. The fact that American technology and management had to be introduced to maintain the French position in computers was a disconcerting fact it had to accept.

Frenchmen, properly regarding their basic scientific capabilities as equal to those of Americans, ascribe the technological leadership of the United States to our huge annual investment in science and technology, and to the rapidity with which American industry converts new knowledge into marketable products. They point to the fact that outlays on scientific research and development—mainly government-financed—are about $24 billion a year in the United States versus less than $2 billion in France. Moreover, American companies have achieved a fleet-footed co-ordination of technological, managerial, and marketing talents that leaves the slower-paced European firm behind.

France has been seeking to narrow the technological gap by several means. Government R and D programs have been expanded. Multinational projects, such as Euratom or the British-French Concorde supersonic transport plane, have been organized to share the huge costs of ambitious undertakings. Cooperation has been sought from technologically advanced countries other than the United States. During his 1966 journey to the Soviet Union, General de Gaulle significantly emphasized scientific co-operation between France and Russia. It should not be forgotten that U.S. and British denial of nuclear knowledge to France created a deep-seated resentment, along with a desire by France to "go it alone" in science. However, most Europeans who are not Gaullists are convinced that the only effective way for Europe to catch up with the United States is more extensive American aid. One expert said: "Unless America helps us resolve this problem now, it may have to launch another 'Marshall Plan' of technological aid in the 1970's. The U.S. cannot afford to keep all of the marbles in the economic game!"

An important question is whether the U.S. technological lead is increasing or diminishing. Over all, the answer is not clear. While Europe is technically abreast of the United States in chemicals and fertilizers, and is holding its position, in other fields it may be either gaining or losing ground. An American computer expert with long European experience observed that when he first analyzed the state of European computer technology in 1958, he found it to be about eight years behind the United States. Repeating his survey recently, he found the lag had been reduced to four or five years.

Modernization of Management

Despite recent progress and conspicuous exceptions, the management of most French enterprises is still over-centralized, paternalistic, and lacking in scientific attitude. Many firms are family-owned and -operated. Personal connections play a vital role. Under the Patronat—the official organization of French industry—the relations of enterprises to the government are close, and trade organizations play an important role. A web of governmental regulation surrounds the manager. As a result of all these factors, competition is muted.

Like Britain and West Germany, France has been backward in recognizing the need for rigorous advanced education for management. Engineering has been the traditional discipline out of which the majority of French managers have come. Apart from commercial schools focusing upon accounting, and short courses for practicing managers, the French educational system has offered little to prepare young men for managerial careers at the graduate level. This is now changing. Schools of administration and management are being established to supply the talent needed for a growing economy. One is INSEAD at Fontainebleau. The École des Hautes Études Commerciales, a magnificent physical plant for which was recently built in the village of Jouy-en-Josas near Paris, will be another.

As important in the modernization of French management as its new schools is the influence of American corporations doing business in France. Expatriate American managers of French subsidiary or branch enterprises tend to bring with them the fast-moving, hard-hitting practices of their homeland. Naturally, their methods are often viewed askance. There are complaints that the American businessman does not conform to French business customs in his treatment of employees. They engage in the "questionable" practices of cutting prices and invading the traditional markets of their rivals. As a result, French officials have sometimes dragged their feet in approving new American industrial investments.

Nevertheless, there is general agreement that U.S. corporate influence on the French economy has been constructive. Not only has it supplied capital urgently needed to meet investment targets, but it has shaken up French management practices in industries that badly needed it. For example, the Levitt organization, well-known in the United States as a large-scale builder of homes, introduced many innovations into the archaic French residential construction industry through a large French project. Enormous values accrue to any economy from international transmissions of scientific technology and management. They emphasize the need for maximum freedom of international trade and investment.

Improving the Capital Market

Another barrier to future growth of the French economy is lack of a well-developed capital market. Shortage of capital has been a recurrent complaint. This shortage was aggravated by the "voluntary restraint" of foreign investment by American businesses and banks begun in 1964 at the request of the U.S. Government to help reduce the deficit in the U.S. balance of payments. And, in part, it was created by over-ambitious investment plans. To a considerable degree, it reflects faults in the French financial system, which does not yet provide machinery for mobilizing the substantial savings of the public and channeling them efficiently into private investment. France is a rich country, and Frenchmen are traditionally thrifty; but they are wary of investing their money in common stocks. Additional investment banking and underwriting houses are needed, as well as savings and loan institutions to finance home building through long-term amortized loans.

France's Future

Under President de Gaulle, France has grown economically strong, politically stable, and independent. As a result, it has acquired a new mood of confidence and national pride. Gaullists formed less than an absolute majority of the French electorate in 1966 but constituted a politically dominant bloc. They say that their aim is to convert France into a modern nation—to make this ancient country with its 2,000-year history again a power to be reckoned with in the world. Their policy has been reformist and liberal rather than rightist, and it put the Communist Party into disarray. French Communists, offering no attractive alternative to the accomplishments of neo-capitalism in France, have seen their following decline to 20 per cent of the electorate. Increasingly, Frenchmen see that Marxism is an anachronism.

Gaullists say that France had to leave NATO because of the end of U.S. atomic monopoly, the end of colonialism, and the end of monolithic communism. World conditions have changed; the cold war is over. French dissociation from NATO is not a sign of enmity to the United States. Indeed, when the Soviet Union threatened to put its missiles on Cuba, France was the only country that publicly announced its intention to go to war on the U.S. side, if necessary.

We shall not here evaluate these political views. Critics may argue that they are unrealistic, that France is endangering its own interests and threatening the viability of the E.E.C. by insisting upon "go-it-alone" policies. While Americans can take satisfaction from the Gaullist rout of communism in France, they may also feel apprehensive about the lengths to which the French compulsion for national identity and power in the world may go. The only admissible future of Europe is the E.E.C. Frenchmen should remember that nationalism is as anachronistic as Marxism in Western Europe today! Unfortunately, each is still a powerful force.

France, Britain, and the Common Market

France is a keystone in the European Economic Community that was projected by the 1958 Treaty of Rome. The E.E.C. is composed of six nations: France, West Germany, Italy, Belgium, the Netherlands, and Luxemburg. Frenchmen such as Robert Schuman, Jean Monnet, and Robert Marjolin played leading roles in this historic effort, first to bring economic unity to old Europe, and next to extend this unity into the political sphere. As noted previously, France participated fully in the program of progressive reduction of trade barriers among the Six. There is general agreement that participation in the Common Market has been a boon to France, by exposing its industry to continental competition and forcing it to modernize its equipment and management methods. French science and engineering has always been creative and innovative. The Common Market helped France to capitalize on these strengths by providing a wider market for its products, enabling it to realize the economies of scale, and gradually introducing a more risk-taking and forward-looking managerial outlook.

Even after the Fifth Republic of De Gaulle was established in 1958, progress continued toward the tariff and trade goals of the E.E.C. However, the rising nationalistic spirit and the aspirations of Gaullism appeared to many observers to be an impediment to the full economic and political integration of the Six. Would France regard the E.E.C. merely as an instrument to re-establish its leadership of Western Europe? Or would France be willing to take its place as one nation among equals? Apprehension about the answers to these questions was not diminished by De Gaulle's leadership in blocking the entry of Britain into membership in the E.E.C. in 1963, or by the subsequent painful negotiations among the Six for a common agricultural policy. Many supporters of the E.E.C. began to entertain doubts that a community would, in fact, be realized.

One clear conclusion that emerged from discussions with European leaders in 1966 is that the E.E.C. is here to stay. It has made too much progress, and there are already too many vested interests in its success, to permit of a retreat. De Gaulle was surprised at the strength of support of the E.E.C. by the people in the 1965 French elections. Even the Communist-led trade unions in France and Italy supported it.

At the same time, it is recognized that the E.E.C. is now at the critical point of reaching for true integration of the monetary, fiscal, social security, energy, transportation, and other economic policies of the Six. A customs union was achieved ahead of plan, and should be completed by 1968. Yet progress on other fronts has been lagging. The largest tasks in executing the Treaty of Rome lie ahead. Despite grave difficulties in reconciling national differences in other spheres of economic policy, there is a good probability that they will be surmounted. One reason for hope is that the elimination of differences in one area creates pressure for eliminating them in other areas. For example, the leveling of tariff barriers to internal trade has generated pressure to reconcile differences in national tax systems that now bear unequally on exporters and importers in the Six. As national tax systems become more similar, they will tend to narrow the divergencies between social security and other government expenditure programs. And so on.

Apart from the problem of maintaining the forward momentum of the E.E.C., there is the task of enlarging it. Here one confronts two questions. Why did France oppose the entry of Britain in 1963? Under what conditions would Britain be accepted? Many Europeans—including Belgians and Germans as well as Frenchmen—respond that Britain was not ready for E.E.C. membership in 1963. They cite two impediments, one economic and one political. First, there was doubt that Britain could have met the economic expansion goals of the E.E.C., given its persistent deficit in balance of international payments, the weakness of the pound, and the slow rise in productivity in British industry. Second, there was doubt that Britain was prepared to meet the political integration goals of the E.E.C., considering its ties to the Commonwealth and the "special relation" it has maintained with the United States. Britain must choose between Europe and America. It must put its own economy in order before it could become an effective partner in the E.E.C.

Britain has renewed its application for admission to the E.E.C. The chances are that it will meet with an affirmative response, this time or next, *provided* that the governments of the Six are convinced that Britain will be "a good European" and that it is making measurable progress toward a more dynamic economy. It remains to be seen whether the austerity program put into effect by Prime Minister Wilson during 1966 marks the beginning of an enduring improvement in Britain's balance of payments, in the strength of the pound, and in economic vigor. Additional and more powerful remedies, including devaluation, may have to be applied. Whether Europeans, and particularly Gaullists, can be persuaded that Britain is really opting for the European Community and ending its special commitments and ties to America and the Commonwealth countries is also conjectural. France will sponsor British admission as soon as it is convinced that Britain is *in* Europe—not merely *of* Europe. It demands a change in British attitudes, typified by the tongue-in-cheek headline in a British newspaper which read: "Fog over Channel: Continent Isolated!"

Certainly West Germany and the Benelux countries would apply less rigorous standards to British entry than France. They would welcome British influence in the E.E.C. as a counterpoise to the threat of French dominance; but not, of course, at the price of British dominance. There was some apprehension that Britain's entry might slow the Community's progress toward political integration. However, this prospect might not be displeasing to the Gaullists, who might for that reason reduce the "price" charged Britain for its membership.

Selected Sources and References for Chapter 3

Ambassade de France, Service de Presse et d'Information. *France and Economic Planning*. New York: April 1963.

————. *A Balance Sheet of the Main Reforms under the Fifth Republic of France*. New York: March 1966.

Barach, Arnold B. *The New Europe and Its Economic Future*. Washington: Twentieth Century Fund, 1964.

Dewhurst, J. Frederic; Coppock, John O.; Yates, P. Lamartine; *et al. Europe's Needs and Resources*. New York: Twentieth Century Fund, 1961.

Kindleberger, Charles P. "French Planning," in *Conference on Economic Planning*. New York: National Bureau of Economic Research, November 1964.

Lutz, Vera. *French Planning*. Washington: American Enterprise Institute for Public Policy Research, May 1965.

————. "The French 'Miracle,' " in *Economic Miracles*. London: Published for the Institute of Economic Affairs by André Deutsch, Ltd., 1964.

Svennilson, Ingvar. *Growth and Stagnation in the European Economy*. Geneva: United Nations Economic Commission for Europe, 1954.

4. Germany: Restructuring After the "Miracle"

The phoenixlike rise of West Germany from the ashes of utter defeat in World War II has often been described as a *wirtschafts-wunder*. In 1945 Germany lay prostrate. Millions of its young men were dead or in prison camps. Much of its industry and housing was reduced to piles of rubble. Its currency was no longer used in trade. Split into four zones that were occupied by allied powers holding widely different views about reconstruction —or whether industrial revival should even be permitted—Germany's economy stagnated.

Twenty years later, West Germany had one of the world's strongest economies. Its total annual output exceeded that of Britain or France, and was surpassed only by the gross products of the United States, the U.S.S.R., and Japan. West Germans enjoyed nearly the highest standard of living in Europe. The

Deutschemark was a hard currency, backed by a gold reserve of over $5 billion. West German goods moved into world markets in a total volume exceeding even that of Britain, the traditional citadel of international trade. All this had been accomplished under an economic policy that rejected state economic planning, offered powerful incentives to work, enterprise and capital accumulation, and was based mainly upon impersonal regulation by competitive markets.

Yet, in the early sixties the fast-paced Germany economy began to show signs of getting winded. After growing at an average annual rate of more than 7.6 per cent during the period 1950–1963, real GNP rose only 4.4 per cent during 1965 and an estimated 3.8 per cent during 1966. The coal and steel industries—pillars of the economy—were deep in competitive trouble. Shortages of capital and high interest rates were bottlenecks to further industrial expansion. Labor shortages were producing hefty increases in pay that outstripped the average rise in labor productivity. Government spending programs, including those to carry out Western Europe's most comprehensive social security program, were creating deficits that fanned the fires of price inflation. The cost-of-living index in mid-1966 was up 4.2 per cent over its level a year earlier, raising an ominous specter from the past in the minds of inflation-conscious Germans.

The visitor to Germany in the mid-sixties, familiar with these facts, sought answers to a number of questions. What were the real sources of the *wirtschaftswunder?* Were the postwar forces that were behind the country's fast growth playing out? If so, what new factors, if any, could prolong its progress? In particular, did the character of West German economic policy contribute to past economic performance? Were changes likely to be made in this policy to meet new internal and environmental conditions? What were German attitudes toward the Common Market and its enlargement to include Britain and other European countries? Did the reunification of the two Germanies continue to bulk large in West German thinking? How could the structures and policies of two economies now so dissimilar as those of the western Federal Republic of Germany (FRG) and the eastern German Democratic Republic (GDR) be harmonized, even assuming that formidable political barriers could be surmounted?

Explaining the "Miracle"

Germany's surrender in World War II was followed by three desperate and economically wasted years. Under the Potsdam Agreement of July–August 1945, the three victorious powers (France did not participate although it was later assigned a zone of occupation) agreed upon policies of decentralization and de-industrialization of the Germany economy. They concurred in the cession of all German territory east of the Oder-Neisse rivers to Poland; this was about 23 per cent of German territory as constituted by the Treaty of Versailles in 1919. This promptly drove millions of Germans westward, adding to the turmoil of reconstruction. In March 1946 the Allied powers announced a plan to limit German industry to 50 per cent of its 1938 level. The Soviet Union removed immense quantities of industrial equipment from its East German zone as war reparations. Rising friction between the U.S.S.R. and the Western powers over oc-cupation policies led the United States and Britain to establish a unified Bizone during 1947 for administrative purposes. In the same year the Western allies abandoned the "cabbage-patch" concept of the German economy as inhuman and unrealistic, raised the limits upon industrial growth, and later removed them altogether. A German Economic Council was entrusted with powers to guide economic reconstruction.

The year 1948 marked a turning point in Germany's history. The three Western powers agreed to unify their zones of occupa-tion under a new German government headed by Konrad Ade-nauer, whose minister of economics was Ludwig Erhard, the vigorous exponent of market economics. (The Soviet reaction was to blockade Berlin against the West, and in the following year to cause the establishment of the GDR in its East German zone of occupation.) In June 1948 upon the initiative of the Western allies a new currency, the Deutschemark, was intro-duced, with 6.5 new units equivalent to 100 of the old reichs-marks in cash or on deposit. Henceforth, in the words of Erhard, "the only ration coupon is the mark." Currency reform was harsh on people with fixed incomes; but its effects were mitigated by social security, and it stimulated business powerfully. Concur-rently, direct economic controls were lifted. Meanwhile, expanded American economic aid under the Marshall Plan began to relieve want and to provide the fuel and materials for industrial reconstruction. During the second half of 1948, West Germany's industrial production rose from 45 per cent to 75 per cent of its 1936 level.

Erhard has given the following dramatic description of the deadening impact of a functionless currency and direct controls upon the economy: "We endured the phenomenon of a 'price-frozen' inflation. The vast sum of money in circulation prevented any central economic planning. Turnover no longer went through regular wholesale and retail channels, or did so only in small part. Increasingly, goods remained in warehouses, except where they could be used in compensatory transactions and so sustain business on a small scale. We had returned to a primitive state of barter." After currency reform and the removal of controls: "The black market suddenly disappeared. Shop windows were full of goods. Factory chimneys were smoking. The streets swarmed with lorries. Everywhere the noise of new buildings going up replaced the deathly silence of the ruins."

The year 1949 witnessed the completion of the split between West and East Germany. The epic Anglo-American airlift relieved Berlin, and the blockade was lifted by the Soviet Union in May 1949. The Western Allies thereupon gave over political control of West Berlin to a new government under Ernst Reuter. Concurrently, a Joint Occupation Statute transmitted nearly full powers of government to the FRG, which immediately launched a program to stimulate growth under private enterprise and competitive markets. Meanwhile, the Soviet-dominated GDR nationalized the industries of East Germany, redistributed land to the tenants, and inaugurated Soviet-style state planning of the economy.

The economic consequences of the separation of the two Germanies were mixed. West Germany no longer could obtain important food supplies from the East, and was forced to expand exports of manufactured goods to earn the foreign exchange to buy food elsewhere. More important, an enormous stream of refugees from Poland and East Germany moved westward— some 13 million people between 1945 and 1960. This huge supply of labor entered West Germany in desperate need of employment, willing to accept low wages and to forego the privilege of striking. In addition, women unable to marry because of wartime manpower losses took jobs.

More than a swelling supply of cheap and skilled labor was involved in the explosive rise of West German production. Between 1950 and 1960 production *per head* of the working population rose 5.8 per cent a year, more than double the rise in the United States or the United Kingdom. What made output per man-hour rise so rapidly in West Germany was not only the diligence of a trained and needy population, offered strong incentives to work and to increase its income, but also a high annual rate of gross fixed capital formation that averaged 22 per cent of the GNP during 1953–1960. This was more than one third higher than in the United States and the United Kingdom. The German worker's efforts were thus fructified by a rapidly improving supply of power, machines, and tools. The FRG kept income taxes low on business profits, leaving a large share available for plowing back into new plant and equipment. Workers were encouraged to work long hours by the exemption of overtime earnings and various forms of savings from the personal income tax.

Although some disagree, the keys to the "miracle" apparently were, first, currency reform and decontrol, and second, the economic policies of the FRG and the philosophy that lay behind them. The central policy, originally advanced by Professor Walter Eucken and his University of Freiburg school, was that of the *soziale marktwirtschaft* or responsible free-market economy. This was an economy in which the major aim of the state was to maximize individual freedom, and in which competition in markets rather than regulation by government officials would determine prices, private spending, and private investment. The emphasis placed by Erhard upon competitive private enterprise was, in part, a reaction against the interventionism of Hitler's Nazi regime. It was also in polar opposition to state central planning in Eastern Europe.

The *soziale marktwirtschaft* was by no means a throwback to the economic "Darwinism" or laissez-faire concepts of the nineteenth century. It contemplated an active role for the state. The state should encourage a full-employment level of aggregate demand by fiscal and monetary measures, should enforce the competitive rules of the game, should lessen income inequalities through progressive taxation, and should put a floor of personal welfare under the individual through a comprehensive social-security system. Within this government-created environment, the individual had the opportunity—and responsibility—to improve his condition by his own choices and efforts. These ideas appealed to most West Germans.

A central concern of the German Government after 1948 was monetary and fiscal stability. The recollections of the chaos caused by hyperinflation of the currency in two world wars made the German people highly sensitive to rising prices. No price, not even unemployment, was too large to pay for a mark of stable buying power. The FRG used a restrictive but flexible monetary policy to keep the price level down. The cost of living in the FRG rose only moderately until the early sixties, when heavy government spending and cost-push forces began to appear. Indeed, anti-inflationary policies during the fifties were so much more effective in West Germany than in other European countries that booming exports resulted in large surpluses in the balance of payments, a piling up of monetary reserves, and, in 1961, an *upward* revaluation of the mark!

Prosperity and New Problems

In the mid-sixties the FRG exemplified many aspects of an affluent society. Its 1965 GNP of $112 billion, produced by a population of about 60 million people, gave it a GNP, per capita, of $1,870—one of the highest in the world. The factories of the Ruhr Valley were throbbing and smoking with activity. With 650,000 unfilled jobs, a state of overemployment prevailed, despite the fact that 1.2 million of "guest *arbeiters*" from southern Europe had been brought in to augment the labor force. Automobiles and trucks jammed the wide autobahns. Stores were well stocked with an abundance of consumer goods. The sidewalk cafés of West Berlin, Düsseldorf, and Frankfurt were crowded with well-garbed patrons. The farms and villages were neat and opulent. Although housing and living space continued to be tight, wartime damage was almost completely repaired, and the average German and his family lived spaciously compared to his East European counterpart.

But it was clear in 1966 that the *wirtschaftswunder* was over. The long postwar boom had ended in 1963, and the growth rate of real GNP had declined successively thereafter. There was abundant evidence that economic progress in the future would be slower. The sweeping advances of 1948–1963 had been dependent primarily upon reconstruction, the utilization of modern technology and equipment in the expansion of traditional industries, and a burgeoning labor force. Some $4.4 billion of U.S. and British aid had speeded the reconstruction during 1946–1951, and liberal investment by private foreign enterprises thereafter had helped to foster growth. An apparent limitless supply of efficient labor had been available from domestic sources, from German refugees from the East, and from southern Europe. A relatively light burden of national defense had freed domestic resources for public and private investment.

Most of these growth forces were weakening or disappearing. The bottom of the manpower barrel had been reached. Foreign investment was diminishing as a result of U.S. restrictions. German costs were rising faster than in the United States and many European countries, as labor unions demanded an increasing share of the social product. This put a crimp in exports. The coal and steel industries had entered a critical period. The FRG was being required to carry a larger share of its defense burden. Local capital for business expansion was limited as a result of burgeoning public expenditure programs, high interest rates, and a poorly organized capital market. New wellsprings of growth had to be found. An industrial restructuring of the economy had become necessary. Above all, new policies were needed to guide an economy for which the simple and direct prescriptions of the *soziale marktwirtschaft* no longer sufficed. West Germany had entered a new era, and uncertainty pervaded the business community.

The salient problems confronting the nation can be recapitulated under the headings of manpower, capital, management, coal, steel, Ruhr redevelopment, and the Common Market. We now turn to the measures proposed to resolve them.

Refilling the Manpower Barrel

The great westward trek of Germans from the East virtually ended in 1961 with the erection of the infamous Berlin Wall and other measures of the GDR to stabilize its labor force. (Until the wall went up, an East German factory manager never knew what personnel would report for work the next day!) Thereafter, more than a million "guest *arbeiters*" were induced to move into the FRG from southern Italy, and from Spain, Turkey, and Greece. This immigration, too, virtually ceased by 1966, because of rapidly improving employment opportunities in the countries of origin.

Although they had relieved the labor shortage, foreign workers were a costly resource. They presented problems of social assimilation, and required their employers to make large investments in training, language instruction, and housing. Housing, especially, had been a serious problem in a densely populated country with fantastically high land prices. In the future, the native population would be the sole source of additional labor, and the rate of new entrants would be relatively low during the next decade because of the World War II "baby gap."

Recognizing that Germany's fate depends upon industrial expansion, its leaders planned to augment its labor supply by shifting inefficiently employed workers out of agriculture and coal mining. Agriculture could be the source of one million additional factory workers within eight to ten years. Since 1950, some 150,000 miners had left the coal pits, and another 100,000 of the remaining 350,000 could leave by 1970. Bold manpower relocation and retraining programs were contemplated. In addition, manpower could be released for more efficient employment by mechanization of industrial processes. The elimination of tariff barriers within the Common Market, and between it and the external world, could also help.

Another solution to the West German manpower shortage was to shift labor-intensive production from Germany to Eastern Europe, the Mediterranean countries, and less-developed regions, while keeping it under German management. Such a marriage of German technical and managerial skills with low-cost foreign labor could be very productive. West German firms had already established labor-intensive plants making cutlery, veneered furniture, and shirts in Ghana, Liberia, and India. Krupp had shifted production of many of its truck parts to Poland, which exported them to West Germany for assembly into the finished vehicle. However, this solution to the manpower shortage—like the problems of automation and internal redistribution of the labor force—would require immense amounts of capital not yet clearly in sight. It would also be time consuming.

Relieving the Capital Shortage

Tight money and high interest rates always bite deeply into the plans of enterprises or nations that are in process of rapid expansion. West Germany is no exception to this rule. Burgeoning investment by business firms, combined with heavy capital spending programs by German governments, outran the available supply of domestic savings and drove the costs of capital to high levels. Firms formerly able to finance their expansion through retained profits found that shrinking margins and heavier taxes compelled them to make use of banks and capital markets. In 1966, interest rates on business loans of good quality were 9 to 10 per cent a year. To restrain the price inflation that developed during the mid-sixties, monetary policy had become severely restrictive. Many public and private projects were being postponed, either because they could not be financed or because they were uneconomic with the high costs of capital. Meanwhile, the inflow of foreign investment was curtailed. What policies could the Government introduce to alleviate the capital shortage, and to augment the volume of industrial investment upon which the efficiency of German industry and its competitive position in world markets depended?

Two approaches were being developed: to improve the functioning of German capital markets; and to raise taxes, put government spending on a pay-as-you-go basis, and reduce governmental competition with private enterprises for the savings of the public. Germany lacks financial institutions capable of mobilizing savings and transmuting them efficiently into productive private investment. Its leaders recognize that the establishment of an apparatus of financial intermediation is a first order of business. This implies broadening public ownership of shares in business, raising standards of corporate accounting and reporting and—above all—maintaining public confidence in a stable mark.

To make private capital markets work effectively requires a fiscally responsible government. Rising prosperity led to heavy increases in governmental expenditures, particularly for social-security benefits, housing and agricultural subsidies, and grants to the coal and shipping industries. Budget deficits added to inflationary pressures and put the government in competition with private industry for loans. Erhard's answer was to reduce public spending and increase taxes. Fiscal rigor is never popular, and the replacement of his Government by one headed by Kurt Kiesinger late in 1966 put the future course of German fiscal policy in doubt.

Upgrading Management and Rationalizing Industry

Along with labor and capital, a supply of competent management is a condition of economic growth. German industrial managers have always been technically proficient and energetic. Traditionally, their formal academic training has been in science, in engineering, or in commercial schools that emphasized accounting. There has not been a single graduate school of management in a German university—a serious deficiency that must be remedied. The labor shortage has caused a drive to mechanize and automate distribution and service industries as well as manufacturing. Scientific methods of capital budgeting have taken on new significance. Shrinking profit margins and complex problems of labor and community relations have made German firms more conscious of the need for professionally trained managers. American management consulting firms have become increasingly active.

As in France, U.S. business penetration has been helpful in modernizing the attitudes and practices of German management. By the end of 1965, American firms had invested about $2 billion in West Germany, embracing some 400 industrial establishments that collectively accounted for about 5 per cent of Germany's industrial capital and employed about 1 per cent of its labor force. In general, American investment was concentrated in growth industries like petroleum, autos, tires, computers, and electronics. American management was introducing new sales techniques and merchandising institutions, such as shopping centers, supermarkets, discount houses, and mail-order chain stores. It was stimulating research and development. It was also helping to create sharper competition. "Understandings" within German industries regarding prices and market shares were being destroyed. New concepts of market strategy were brought in. For example, Owens-Illinois purchased control of a German old-line manufacturer of glass bottles. Shortly thereafter, it introduced plastic bottles, to the consternation of a German glass bottle industry that was unfamiliar with the concept of a *container* market strategy.

As might be expected, the entry of U.S. branches and subsidiaries provoked complaints about "unfair competition," worsening the German balance of payments by profit remittances to the United States, and wage inflation as a result of the higher pay offered by American firms. Germans have also been critical of acquisitions of their firms by U.S. corporations *with German funds*—such as the acquisition of Deutsche Erdol by Texaco—largely by means of securities floated within Germany. However, they have generally been less resistant to U.S. industrial penetration than the French and have realized that restrictive policies against U.S. investment would only tend to perpetuate the technological gap between American and German industry.

Another adaptation to the new conditions of the sixties is enlargement of German enterprises. The squeeze on profit margins, combined with the larger opportunities offered by the Common Market, has produced a wave of mergers and combinations. These are bound to continue, as more firms seek to gain the competitive advantages of optimum scale. Mergers enable the enlarged enterprise to specialize each of its plants to longer production runs of particular products, thus lowering production costs per unit. Marketing costs per unit fall as sales promotion outlays are spread over a larger volume. Larger and more productive research and development programs become possible.

Unlike France, which has had a national policy to promote combinations, the FRG left the process to the working of market forces.

Is there a danger that mergers will lead to undue concentration of industry or to the revival of the cartels? Probably not. The merger movement should be viewed as a desirable adjustment of a national industrial structure to the emergence of a continental market in Europe. It is the counterpart of the U.S. merger movement early in the present century, which realized the advantages of scale in serving the continental market then opening up. Whether mergers will lead to an undue concentration of European industry and monopolistic behavior in the future depends largely upon the height of the external tariff wall erected around the E.E.C. If, as one hopes, it is kept low, U.S.

and other foreign firms will keep European business behavior competitive. Also, it should be remembered that cartels were explicitly outlawed by the Treaty of Rome, although there were some loopholes.

Rumblings in the Ruhr

Coal is Germany's only large natural resource, and coal mining has been a basic industry since the mid-nineteenth century. Yet coal mining has become a "sick" industry with no prospect of getting well, because of the relatively high cost of German coal and growing competition with oil and gas in the European energy market. Beyond this, the generally thin and discontinuous seams of German mines must be worked deep underground, under conditions that do not permit of thorough mechanization. German coal cannot compete with mechanically-produced U.S. coal, which can be laid down in the Ruhr Valley at $4 per ton less than the German cost. The sharp postwar shift from coal to petroleum as an energy source in Europe has amplified the crisis. Coal stocks have piled up, production schedules have been cut back, and many German miners confront permanent unemployment. Having liberally subsidized the coal industry in the past, the German government now accepts the need for a shift of manpower out of the industry. Massive retraining and relocation programs for miners are being launched.

Steel is another traditional pillar of the German economy that has fallen on evil days. Unlike coal, steel's problems are curable. German steel costs have risen relative to those of other countries because of high-cost German coal and the booming wages of labor. Also, steel-making technology has been undergoing rapid changes, and recently built mills have a large competitive advantage. In 1966, leading German steel companies claimed to be operating at a loss, as a consequence of fierce competition with Japanese, Belgian, French, and Italian steel. The answers to these problems must be modernization of German steel-making plant and equipment, and efforts to hold down wage increases. The German steel industry probably will not recover its competitive strength without a period of unemployment.

The plight of German coal and steel is the crux of the problem of the Ruhr Valley. The Ruhr is the industrial heart of West Germany and, indeed, of Western Europe—a vast metropolitan area containing more than 6 million people. Heavily dependent upon coal and steel production, its future viability is threatened. New industries must be found to employ the skilled and industrious people who will be displaced from industries which are declining. The German government is making efforts to attract growth industries to the Ruhr, by arranging to make plant sites available on favorable terms. No doubt, other measures will be taken as well.

Germany and Its Neighbors

West Germany has been the most dedicated member of the E.E.C. More than any other country except France, it has contributed intellectual leadership to the European Community and has benefited from the expanded market opportunities it created. Germans have naturally been apprehensive about De Gaulle's nationalistic pretensions and their effects upon the E.E.C. German opinion of the E.E.C.'s future was, nevertheless, optimistic. The E.E.C. had passed the point of no return. There were already too many vested interests in economic integration to make a retreat conceivable, even though difficult steps lay ahead. One reason for German optimism was the success attained in solving the most difficult problem so far raised by the Common Market— agricultural policy. It had proved possible to compromise Germany's highly protective farm policies and the more liberal policies of France. For reasons set forth in the last section of the preceding chapter, Germans were confident that the E.E.C. ultimately would be enlarged and a fuller measure of integration achieved.

One issue on which German leaders join with De Gaulle is the desirability of expanding economic relationships with countries east of the Iron Curtain. As a trade-oriented people, West Germans look for business wherever it may be found, irrespective of political differences. They point out that there is no longer a Communist monolith: Yugoslavia, Rumania, Hungary, Poland, and Czechoslovakia are all pursuing their own economic courses with wide variations among them. Even though the FRG does not recognize the Government of the DGR, a flourishing trade has developed between the two Germanies. About 15 per cent of East Germany's trade, and about 5 per cent of West Germany's trade, is involved. In addition, a flow of technology has begun, mainly from West to East. West German firms have entered into joint ventures with enterprises in the Communist countries, under which the Germans supply patents, technology, and manufacturing know-how while the other country supplies labor and capital. West Germans urge the United States to lower its barriers to trade with Eastern Europe.

Although per-capita income in the FRG is much higher than in the GDR, the economic growth of East Germany up to recent years has been comparable to that of its western neighbor. Central planning and Stalinist discipline can get results—up to a point. The GDR adopted a new economic program in 1963 which decentralized authority to enterprise managers, strengthened incentives to workers, and introduced a measure of market pricing of commodities. Thus it thrust ahead of Soviet Russia in modernizing its system of economic guidance. The East German already enjoyed a living standard about 30 per cent higher than the Soviet citizen.

Despite economic liberalization, the GDR maintained more Communist Party discipline and Stalinist police controls than any other Communist country in Europe—probably because of well-founded doubts about the loyalty of the people. This presents an interesting question: Can political repression continue indefinitely, while economic controls are being loosened? The Berlin Wall bears eloquent testimony to communism's inability to command the support of people.

Because West Berlin maintained close economic relations with the FRG, it had a high and sustained growth of output. In 1965 it generated a gross product of $4.5 billion, approximately 4 per cent of the FRG total. Electrical and electronic equipment dominated its industrial production. A substantial part of its exports filled orders placed by the FRG government, making it, in one sense, a subsidized economy. The administration of Berlin has sought to bolster its economy, to prevent attrition of population, and to overcome its locational handicaps by a 30 per cent reduction in income-tax rates and larger depreciation allowances than are applied in West Germany. This policy has attracted many industries, and has stabilized the population and labor force. Industries that need little space and produce for export rather than the local market are preferred, because the city is hemmed in by East German barriers.

There can be no doubt that "the German question"—the unification of the two Germanies—is a priority item on the agenda of the FRG. Nationalism remains a strong force in the world, and, increasingly, Germans are taking initiatives toward reunification. An essay concerned with economic matters is not the place to explore the formidable military and political problems that must be resolved. How an *economic* integration of West and East Germany could be achieved is, however, a pertinent question. Obviously, it would call for an unprecedented effort to harmonize divergent economic policies. One expert observer speculated that East Germany would be willing to give up most direct economic controls, provided that it could maintain its land reform, its nationalized large industries and its state housing, medical and social-security programs. West Germany, in turn, would probably be willing to accept a larger measure of nationalized industry and central planning, provided that basic economic guidance came from competitive markets. Indeed, both countries had already moved a few steps during the 1960's to close the economic-policy gap.

Prospects for Future Growth

West Germany in the mid-1960's was a nation in transition from high to moderate economic growth. Essential changes in both structural and stabilization policies of the FRG will require several years to work out, and important effects of those changes will only appear several years later. Annual increases of about 4 per cent in the national product are likely to characterize the late 1960's and the early 1970's, instead of the 7 to 8 per cent annual gains of the fifties.

The aims of German stabilization policy must be to "cool off" an overheated and overemployed economy threatened with price inflation. Strong monetary restraint must be supplemented by fiscal restraint. The aims of structural policies must be to remove the manpower, capital, and management bottlenecks to future growth. Germany is confronted by the imperative to find new industries to replace those in decline, and to speed up technological changes and managerial competence. Only thus can it maintain the position in world markets so essential to its well-being. These problems were being confronted honestly, and there was hope for their solution.

Selected Sources and References for Chapter 4

Achievement in Figures. Results of the Work of Reconstruction in the Federal Republic of Germany 1949–1962. Bonn: Federal Ministry of Economics, 1963.

Data on West Berlin and Its Economy. Senator for Economy and Credit. Berlin: Schoenberg, 1966.

Erhard, Ludwig. *Prosperity through Competition.* London: Thames and Hudson, 1958.

Hartmann, Heintz. *Authority and Organization in German Management.* Princeton: Princeton University Press, 1959.

Hennessy, Josseleyn. "The German Miracle," in *Economic Miracles.* London: Published for the Institute for Economic Affairs by André Deutsch, Ltd., 1964.

Krengel, Rolf. "Prognosis of Output and Factors of Production of Industry in the Federal Republic of Germany, 1965 and 1970," in *Europe's Future in Figures.* Vol. I, ed. R. C. Geary. Amsterdam: North Holland Publishing Company, 1962.

Spulber, Nicolas. *The Economics of Communist Eastern Europe.* New York: John Wiley and Sons, 1957.

Wallich, Henry. *The Mainsprings of the German Revival.* New Haven: Yale University Press, 1955.

5. Poland: Europe's Janus

In 1966 Poland celebrated its millenary—ten centuries of struggle, betrayal, defeat, dismemberment, rebirth, and hope. Despite the confident tone of the celebration, however, Poland had not reached its millennium; it continued to sit anxiously between East and West, looking both ways, beset with internal conflicts, hoping fervently that the future would be better than the past. Not that the celebration was unjustified—it is a wonder even that there is a Poland today. A brief glance back over those thousand years will explain that wonder.

The Political Accordion

Of all the histories of all the countries examined in this book, that of Poland is the least known in the United States. Having emerged as a nation-state in the tenth century, the first Poland lasted some eight hundred years under several dynasties, notably the Piast and Jagiello. During the years 1772–1796 Poland disappeared from the political map. It was ruthlessly carved up by its larger neighbors—Russia, Prussia, and Austria—which were temporarily united by their fear of France, then the most powerful nation of Europe.

Revived by Napoleon and the ideals of the French Revolution, the second Polish state appeared in 1815. Again short-lived, it was absorbed into Russia in 1831. The leaders of Polish nationalism, including Mickiewicz and Chopin, fled west to Paris. There, for the better part of a century until after World War I, the Polish nation existed only in the hearts of Polish exiles.

Poland's partitioners were defeated in World War I, and, since it served their own purposes, the victorious Western Allies created the third Polish state by carving pieces from the empires of the vanquished. But Woodrow Wilson's principle of self-determination, the political machinations of France, Britain, and Germany, and the confusion about boundaries combined to make the carving difficult. It was not until 1921, after several plebiscites, conferences, and armed conflicts, that all the boundaries were set. In the process, the pretext for World War II was created.

Poland's difficulty was an ancient one. The Piast tradition, viewing Germany as the ultimate enemy, favored conciliation in the east and extension of the nation's boundaries as far west as possible. The Jagiello policy was the opposite: conciliate Germany in the west and thrust Poland eastward as far as possible. The Polish folly is that the compromise between these views was usually to stretch boundaries *both* eastward and westward on the basis of exaggerated dreams of a vanished feudal grandeur. It is the tragedy of Central Europe that, as Norman J. G. Pounds has noted, so many peoples "with long historical memories and little historical sense cling so obstinately" to these illusions.

Because of Germany's defeat in World War I and Russia's weakness, the third Poland emerged in the early twenties as the fourth largest country in Europe, in area and population. Its boundaries were both farther east and west than at any time in her history, except when her neighbors—Russia and Germany—were too weak to prevent it. This should have warned the Poles; for, if Polish history teaches one lesson, it is that neither neighbor would long tolerate Polish occupation of lands populated by Russian- or German-speaking peoples. Foolishly, Poland extended its territorial claims as far as possible, hoping that she could hold the balance of power in Central Europe, playing one giant neighbor off against the other.

In the west, the final boundaries of 1919 isolated the vehemently German city of Danzig and the predominantly German area of East Prussia from Germany by the "Corridor." This was a neck of land, predominantly Polish in population, which gave Poland its promised "free and secure access" to the Baltic Sea. By the rule of self-determination Danzig should have become part of German East Prussia; but France and Poland strongly objected and it became, at Lloyd George's suggestion, a "free city." Only twenty years later Hitler invaded Poland on the pretext of coming to the rescue of fellow Germans in western Poland and Danzig.

In the east, Jagiello attitudes caused the 1919 Polish boundaries to be drawn so as to include some 10 million people who were non-Polish in language and attitude. These were Russians, White Russians, Lithuanians, Ukrainians, and Jews who did not consider themselves Poles. The stage was thus set for the Soviet-German pact of August 1939, which triggered the invasion of Poland from the west by German troops and from the east by Russian troops. The third Polish state went into exile and oblivion. Poland was again partitioned and occupied by vengeful neighbors, against whom neither vainglorious feudal claims nor principles of self-determination availed.

The Fourth Polish State

With the end of World War II, the eastern third of prewar Poland was lost for the indefinite future to the Soviet Union. At Soviet insistence, Poland was shifted violently and bodily westwards. To compensate Poland and punish Germany, the western boundary was "tentatively" established along the Oder-Neisse rivers, far into what anyone but a Pole would call modern Germany, with the Polish frontier only fifty miles from Berlin! The Piast stance—alliance with Russia and enmity toward Germany—now dominated Polish policy.

As usual, the major powers could not agree on Poland's western boundary. They accepted the Soviet-sponsored Oder-Neisse line temporarily, giving the Warsaw government administrative authority over the disputed areas. Today, Poland's western boundaries are in legal limbo, with West Germany, Britain, and the United States questioning the Oder-Neisse line and the Poles and Soviets asserting it. This is an important issue. As long as the Federal Republic of Germany refuses to recognize the Oder-Neisse line, the Poles must fear a revival of a militaristic Germany with revanchist ambitions in the east. This cannot but increase Poland's military and political dependence on the Soviet Union. Whether justified or not, Polish anxiety about her western boundary is a major deterrent to a more independent path within the Communist bloc. An independent Poland is just as important for political stability in Central Europe today as ever. Yet, West Germany's attitude toward the boundary question—supported by the United States—forms an impediment to that independence.

The westward shift in 1945 cost Poland 70,000 square miles of territory (20 per cent of prewar) and over 10 million people (30 per cent) in the east, and it gained in the west 39,000 square miles and 8 million people. But these figures are misleading. Many of the inhabitants lost were non-Polish to begin with (Germans, Lithuanians, and others). Also, the lands gained from Germany in the west were far more valuable economically than those lost to Russia in the east. In exchange for rather poor agricultural land in the east, Poland gained lands which were better for agriculture and which included important industrial areas. While remaining essentially an agricultural country, Poland gained an industrial potential which would make it easier to achieve a balanced economy. Poland was more than compensated and, as the Soviets planned, could become a strong buffer against a revived Germany.

Occupied by the Russians as the Germans were pushed back, Poland found itself at the end of World War II with two governments. The one in exile in London was the direct descendant of the prewar government of Pilsudski-Mosciski-Beck; the one in Lublin in eastern Poland was a creation of the Russians. There was no question of the outcome. The Soviets officially recognized the Lublin committee and delivered civil affairs to it. After nominal representation from London was added, Britain and the United States also recognized the Lublin government. Under harsh Soviet-patterned Communist discipline, the task of postwar reconstruction began. The 1947 elections, labeled fraudulent by some, established the Communists firmly in control with 90 per cent of the vote. Bierut became President, Cyran-kiewicz, Prime Minister. Gomulka, Secretary-General of the Polish Communist party, was shortly thereafter purged and imprisoned by the Stalinists who controlled both the Party and the Government.

After Stalin's death in 1953 there was some relaxation of the ruthless police state that had been imposed on Poland. This loosening of control reached a climax with the Poznan riots of 1956. The Stalinists wanted to reinstitute total repression; others urged further relaxation of police control. Despite a hurried trip to Warsaw by Khrushchev, the "liberals" won out. Gomulka was freed and assumed control of the Government. With the assistance of Cardinal Wyszynski, the Government cautiously moved toward greater freedom and defiance of Moscow, thus avoiding further popular uprisings which surely would have invited massive countermeasures by the Russians.

Since 1956 the "thaw" has continued. Intellectuals and others enjoyed more freedom than their counterparts in most other Communist countries of Eastern Europe, although the degree of that freedom fluctuated as Moscow-Warsaw relations changed temperature. In the mid-sixties Poland was still a Communist police state, the Soviet Union was its closest ally, and Red Army troops were still garrisoned in the country.

But Poland was also an overwhelmingly Roman Catholic country. The Church is a vital social and political force that serves to curb the power of the Communist state. Nowhere in Eastern Europe is the Church so strong as in Poland. The identification of Poles with Rome dates from the emergence of Poland as a nation a thousand years ago. The Catholic Church in Poland successfully resisted the Reformation and the wave of Protestantism that swept over Europe in the sixteenth century. It also became closely identified with Polish nationalism and with the persecution of minorities, especially Orthodox Christians and Jews. (The reduction of Poland's Jewish population from 2.7 million in 1931 to about 100,000 after the war was not due exclusively to the actions of Nazi Germany.)

In the interwar period a concordat with the Vatican brought about a very close relationship between Church and state. It was inevitable that there would be deep and unyielding conflict after World War II, when the Communists seized power. There was high drama in 1956 when Gomulka and Cardinal Wyszynski found common cause against the Soviets. Today, the preponderant majority of Poles, devout and active Church members, live in a society run by the Communist Party whose membership includes only 5 per cent of all adult Poles. Confrontation between the two is omnipresent, and not infrequently erupts in physical violence. The larger result of the Church's strength, however, is that it makes Poland less a monolithic Communist society—more like the diverse, pluralistic systems of the West.

Economic Recovery and Development, 1945–1966

In the interwar years, Poland moved steadily toward more economic planning. By 1939 it had a mixed economy, partly socialist, partly capitalist. The fortunes of war then thrust it firmly into the Soviet bloc, with all the apparatus of doctrinaire Communism. The postwar government followed the Soviet model assiduously: nationalization of industry (ostensibly down to three-man enterprises, at one time); land reform and destruction of the large landed estates; obliteration of most private capital and wealth; suppression of consumer in favor of capital goods; and so on. A totalitarian police state insured that the economic model would be followed.

Before the war, Poland faced four major economic problems: rural overpopulation, industrial underdevelopment, development of urban areas, and need for expanded foreign trade. With the second highest birth rate in Europe, the "Malthusian devil" was very real in Poland. At least a quarter of the population lived at starvation levels. Six years of war and awesome destruction created immediate postwar conditions that were appalling. The establishment of a Communist Government with the goal of spreading new ideologies and methods at any cost added to the difficulties.

To the Government there was no more important task, however, than the resettlement of millions of people so as to strengthen Poland's claims on its newly gained western territories. Millions of Germans emigrated from the territories—partly because they wanted to live in a German state and partly because they feared the Poles. Millions of Poles moved in. Of the nearly 9 million people in these areas before the war, fewer than a million were Polish. By the mid-sixties, Germans numbered less than 1 per cent. Although some of the Polish immigrants were resettled from eastern lands lost to the Soviet Union, most were settlers from other parts of Poland, lured westward by economic opportunity. One consequence, of course, was that the new population was a relatively young one. This, in turn, meant a very high birth rate, and the population in the western regions is now rising more through natural increase than immigration.

The pressure of population in a largely agricultural country has long been a Polish problem. Very high birth rates before World War II declined substantially in the postwar period— from 35 to 20 per thousand. The Government actively encouraged population control measures, including voluntary abortion; and resistance on religious grounds diminished. Nonetheless, the rate of population increase—now about 1.2 per cent per annum—has not fallen as rapidly as would be expected from the sharp decline in births, because the death rate has also fallen rapidly.

More dramatic changes have been the increasing urbanization and industrialization of the economy. Half of the people now live in towns, and only one third are supported in agriculture. This double shift has been an important factor in postwar Poland's rapid growth. From 1948 to 1963 the reported increase in real national income averaged a high 10 per cent, and in per capita terms, 8 per cent.

If one measures growth from 1950, on the ground that the late forties were years of reconstruction and recovery, the annual rise of real national income was about 7 per cent. After 1958, the rate declined to about 5 per cent, according to official figures. Industrial production expanded over 12 per cent a year, construction nearly 15 per cent, and agriculture at 4 per cent during the 1948–1963 period. Major strides were made in developing the electric power, steel, chemical, fertilizer, cement, textile, and machine-building industries. An impressive construction program helped to house the growing urban populations.

Four Postwar Stages

There were four distinct periods in postwar Poland's economic development. The first, 1947–1950, was one of reconstruction from the extensive damage of the war. Only the Soviet Union and Yugoslavia suffered more physical damage than Poland. Warsaw was 90 per cent destroyed. The economic problems of recovery, aside from clearing away rubble and feeding a starving population, were formidable. The Three-Year Plan adopted in 1947 set these economic priorities: agricultural implements, machinery and fertilizers; coal; electric energy and electrification; and transportation. What was left of the railroads was oriented to prewar political geography, and a transportation system to serve the new Poland had to be built from the ground up. Agriculture was in disarray and its productivity barely high enough to support the rural population, much less the urban. The new Government broke up the great estates and distributed the land among its peasant tillers. Finding capital for industrial expansion and development of export capacity was also an urgent need.

The second period, 1951–1953, was a period of intense investment and industrial development. Consumption was severely repressed: even official documents talk about *lowered* per capita consumption! National income rose 8.0 per cent annually against a 4.8 per cent average growth of consumption and a 17.2 per cent rise in net investment.

The third period, 1954–1962, was marked by a continued high but declining rate of growth in national income, and by a marked rise in consumption at the expense of investment. This was the period of the Poznan bread riots, widespread discontent, and the subsequent liberalization under Gomulka. Consumption rose from 66 per cent of national income in 1953 to 70 per cent in 1957—a very substantial increase, some of which was supported by growing imports.

During the fourth period, since 1963, the Poles have had to face a well-known dilemma. Continued fast growth of output at the rate desired by the Government required a high rate of capital investment, and therefore a slower growth of consumption than the public would tolerate. There have been two results, each easily observed in Poland today: inflation, and a quest for greater economic efficiency. Inflation is most apparent in the overvalued zloty, the official currency, for which the black-market rate is several times the official one. The Government has made determined and more or less successful efforts to control the hyperinflation of the early postwar period. (The United Nations estimate of the cost-of-living index on a 1937 base was 10,650 in September 1946!) Eventually Poland will have to follow Yugoslavia's lead and free its currency from controls. This step lies several years in the future, however.

Decentralization and Market Socialism

The other response to the conflict of desires for both more growth and more current consumption has been a search for more efficient ways of guiding the economy. As in the Soviet Union, Polish leaders are discovering that, while total planning may work for a while, it becomes grossly inefficient as the economy matures and increases in complexity. They recognize that modifications must be made in their present centralized planning approach, if the country is to make maximum progress. Decisions on the allocation of scarce capital are becoming increasingly important, and central planning does not provide good answers

Polish leaders are looking toward a "market socialism" model, with wider use of market guidance and of profits as an incentive to enterprises, in order to bring about improvements in the range and quality of goods and services. Indeed, Oskar Lange, a distinguished Polish economist and one-time Minister of Finance, was a leading exponent of this idea. More and more decisions are being delegated by the central planners to the managers of individual enterprises. Price and rent controls are being relaxed to permit a closer approach to free market levels. The official bureaucracy appears to be in advance of Soviet Russia in its reforms of economic policy, but behind some of its bloc neighbors.

At the same time, Polish economic leaders believe that central planning was an important if not indispensable instrument during the early postwar period. They propose to continue national economic planning, while gradually introducing more market guidance into the economy. They stress that socialism is not rigid; it is a developing, changing system. They see no inconsistency between socialism and the wide use of market forces in directing resources and enforcing efficiency.

East or West?

East or West. Russia or Germany. Central planning or capitalism. Poland, Janus-like, for centuries has been looking in both directions, seeking the best future for itself. Since World War II it has been firmly committed to Russia, and only the naive would expect Poland to leave the Soviet orbit in the foreseeable future.

On the other hand, strong pressures are turning Poland's head again to the West. Partly, this is a result of its strong historical associations with the West, particularly with France and the United States; partly, it is the ancient Polish suspicion of their fellow Slavs in Moscow; and partly, it is the influence of the Roman Catholic Church. And there are also economic reasons: Poland has historically found in the West the major markets for its own products and sources of supply for commodities it needs.

The pull of trade with the West is very strong in Poland, although two-thirds of its trade today is with other Soviet-bloc countries. The Soviet Union alone has 30–35 per cent of Poland's foreign trade. Poland needs petroleum products, machinery, transportation equipment, and consumer durables. In return, it offers manufactured goods as well as the traditional coal and foodstuffs. An industrializing country needs to trade manufactured goods with other industrial countries. Despite its membership in the Council for Mutual Economic Assistance (COMECON)—the Communist response to the Marshall Plan and the Organization for European Economic Co-operation—Poland is actively seeking more trade with the West as a means of introducing more and better goods into its economy. The United States should respond sympathetically, because a more liberal attitude on our part would benefit both countries.

This is a fitting note on which to conclude our overview of Poland in the mid-sixties. Although definitely within the Soviet bloc, Polish economic leadership appeared to be open-minded and pragmatic, with few doctrinaire ties to orthodox Marxism. Long steps have been taken in recent years to liberalize both economic and political processes, and there is every reason to expect this liberalization to continue, although at the moment it is not proceeding as fast as in certain other Eastern European countries. Poland is cautiously looking to the West, and it is in the best interest of the West to respond positively.

Selected Sources and References for Chapter 5

Alton, T. P. *Polish Postwar Economy*. New York: Columbia University Press, 1955.

Bromke, Adam (ed.). *The Communist States at the Crossroads*. New York: Praeger, 1965.

Central Statistical Office of the Polish People's Republic. *Poland in Figures. 1944–1964.* Warsaw: 1964.

Garvy, George. *Money, Banking and Credit in Eastern Europe.* New York: Federal Reserve Bank of New York, 1966.

Montias, John M. *Central Planning in Poland.* New Haven, Conn.: Yale University Press, 1962.

Pounds, Norman J. G. *Poland Between East and West.* Princeton, N.J.: Van Nostrand, 1964.

Taylor, J. *The Economic Development of Poland, 1919–1950.* Ithaca, N.Y.: Cornell University Press, 1952.

6. *Soviet Russia: Marx versus the Market*

In the Soviet Union one meets the hard core, the mother lode, of world Communism. Here is the state whose Great October Revolution in 1917 launched a huge country on a new economic as well as a new political course, and set the stage for subsequent revolutions in one third of the world. As interpreted by Lenin and Stalin, the doctrines of Karl Marx offered new explanations and solutions to man's age-old problems of resource allocation, efficiency, and capital accumulation. In essence, they called for state ownership and operation of almost the entire productive apparatus of the economy, detailed central planning down to the enterprise, and authoritarian political control of all persons to enforce conformance with the dictates of a one-party government.

For more than forty years the Soviet Union made impressive economic gains under socialist central planning, albeit at heavy human costs. Then, beginning in the late fifties, a disconcerting slowdown began. Over all, the loss of momentum was reflected in a decline in the average annual rise in GNP from 6 to 7 per cent during 1950–1959 to about 4.5 per cent during 1961–1965. This change was accompanied by rising ratios of capital to output in industry, a fall-off in labor productivity, and critical shortages in farm production. In detail, it appeared in the form of shoddy goods, unfinished buildings, idle equipment, and excessive inventories. The whole economy displayed insensitivity to new technology and to the expanding demands of Russian consumers.

Why did Soviet economic progress fall off so sharply in the late fifties? There were several causes. A reduction in the standard workweek from 46 to 41 hours reduced the number of man-hours worked. The upward surge of military and space expenditures and foreign aid put a squeeze on Soviet resources, leaving less for industrial investment. Large investments were made in new high-technology industrial plants for fertilizers, plastics, and synthetic fibers, which were very slow to reach capacity production. Above all, experts agree that the system of detailed central planning and control of more than 2 million separate enterprises had become a source of intolerable inefficiency. Even in earlier years, when Communist leaders concentrated on the building-up of basic industries, the economic guidance system was faulty. In a dynamic economy grown large, complex, and diverse, these faults were magnified to a point where they seriously haltered growth.

Soviet political and intellectual leaders began a searching examination of the institutions of their "command economy." As a result, a second revolution began in Russian economic thought. Western ideas entered into discussion. A consensus began to emerge that markets and prices should play a larger role in the management of the economy. A new pragmatism tended to displace doctrinaire Marxism. In general, three main schools of opinion emerged. The conservative school advocated a return to orthodox central planning, improved by the use of mathematical methods and computers. The radical school saw the correct solution in an all-out shift away from central planning to market socialism. The compromise school, which apparently has the support of the present Communist leadership, favored gradual delegation of more authority to enterprise managers and the introduction of more market guidance, but retention of the central planning apparatus, especially for investment decisions. The reforms proposed by Premier Kosygin to the Communist Party Plenum in September 1965 had their intellectual roots in the liberal ideas of Professor E. G. Liberman, in the experiences of Yugoslavia, and in the writings of the socialist market theorist, Oskar Lange.

With this background knowledge in mind, the visitor to the Soviet Union in the mid-sixties naturally sought answers to some basic questions. Were the causes of deterioration in the performance of the Soviet economy in recent years specific or systemic? What changes are occurring in Soviet economic guidance? Can mathematical methods and computers make detailed central planning work? Would the introduction of markets and prices make central planning work better, or replace it altogether? How fast will the Soviet economy grow during the next decade?

Economic Evolution from Nicholas II to Kosygin

Communist propaganda has cultivated the myth that Russia's economic development began in October 1917. Communist policies alone, it alleges, converted an undeveloped country into an advanced industrialized nation in forty years. Nothing could be further from the truth. Warren Nutter's careful study shows that the 5.3 per-cent annual growth of Russian industrial production during the last forty years of the czars was actually higher than during the subsequent forty years under Communism. Even at the turn of the twentieth century, Russia had a productive agriculture with large exports, a basic network of railroads, some metal-working and manufacturing, and, centered on Baku, the world's largest petroleum industry.

It was not lack of economic progress but the stupid insensitivity of the czars to the need for political and economic liberalization that gave the Bolsheviks their opportunity to seize power after Russia's defeat by Germany in World War I. The sterility of czarist leadership was demonstrated when Hindenburg's armies crushed the Russian forces in 1914 at the battles of Tannenberg and the Masurian Lakes. The German Government then arranged to transport Lenin, the leader of the Bolshevik party, in a sealed railroad car from his exile in Switzerland to

Moscow to foment a revolution and form a new government. Ironically, Germany both produced the intellectual messiah of the Russian revolution and financed its executor!

After vanquishing the White Russians in a protracted civil conflict, Lenin turned his attention to economic problems. He quickly recognized that the U.S.S.R. needed capital, modern technology, and management for satisfactory growth.

The crude form of socialism practiced at the beginning, later known as War Communism, had proved disastrous. Famine and shortages of all kinds were endemic. To provide broader incentives to expanded production, Lenin inaugurated the New Economic Policy (NEP) in 1921. Peasant farms and small enterprises were left in private hands. Foreign enterprises were granted concessions on profitable terms to import and operate industrial plants in Russia. Although increasingly criticized by Communist Party theoreticians as an heretical system, the record shows that the NEP did get the Russian economy moving forward again.

As the country made economic progress and as the Communist Party consolidated its political power, Party opposition to the NEP and to the private enterprisers it fostered ("NEP-MEN") grew more vocal. Governmental controls of the economy were gradually centralized. Lenin died in 1924 and was succeeded by Joseph Stalin, the apostle of totalitarianism. The NEP was terminated in 1927, and in the following year the first Five-Year Plan for 1928–1932 went into effect. Stalin launched a massive effort to build up Russia's military strength and heavy industries. The thirty years of his rule were marked by military discipline, the terror of the secret police, and the brutal suppression of dissentient elements. Economic decision-making was highly centralized. The fulfillment of assigned physical output quotas in successive Five-Year Plans was the overriding goal of all economic policy. Consumption was ruthlessly sacrificed to capital accumulation. (These were the years so vividly described by Koestler in *Darkness at Noon.*)

Nevertheless, the Russian economy moved ahead steadily as a result of these policies, the total mobilization of both womanpower and manpower, and the spread of popular education and modern technology. Applied to the abundant natural resources of the Soviet Union, totalitarian methods converted Russia into a formidable industrial power by the time of World War II. The

Germans dealt Russia a fearful blow during the war. Twenty million Russian soldiers and civilians perished, and whole regions were devastated. Yet, under Stalin's harsh regime postwar recovery was rapid.

The death of Stalin in 1953 precipitated a brief struggle for power among the leaders in the Kremlin. The basic *economic* issue was how far the country should shift toward higher consumption—at the expense of growth, of course. Stalin's first successor, Malenkov, apparently moved too fast in this direction. When he was deposed, Khrushchev assumed leadership on a compromise program.

Under Khrushchev, political terror ended and more freedom of dissent and criticism was permitted. The emphasis on heavy industrial investment continued; but housing, consumer goods, and light industries also received attention. The Soviet Union made rapid progress during most of the 1950's. Experts debate the rate of growth achieved in the GNP, and the answer must be uncertain because of differences in national income accounting between the United States and the U.S.S.R. The most defensible estimate is that, up to 1958, the Soviet Union's real gain in GNP averaged 6–7 per cent a year—substantially higher than the 3.3 per cent growth rate attained by the U.S. economy during the same period. This was the era in which Khrushchev confidently promised to "overtake and surpass" the United States by 1970 and to "bury capitalism."

Until 1957 the State Plan was administered by nationwide industrial ministries in Moscow. Over time, each ministry had tended to become as self-sufficient as possible in order to assure itself needed raw materials, labor, and transportation. It practiced "departmentalism," often putting its own bureaucratic interests before those of the country. Large inventories were hoarded to assure against interruption of production which, in turn, might prevent the meeting of the Plan targets by which performance was judged. By-products were not efficiently utilized. New product development and quality improvements were neglected.

In 1957 Khrushchev abolished the industrial ministries, and assigned their functions to 105 regional economic councils—the sovnarkozy. Each sovnarkoz was charged with executing the national Plan within its region. Long-term as well as short-term planning was again vested in GOSPLAN—the central planning commission—which co-ordinated the plans of the sovnarkozy as submitted through the governments of the fifteen republics of the U.S.S.R. While this radical reorganization did bring economic decision-making powers closer to the scene of operations, the new system developed its own defects. The undependability of needed raw materials, labor, and transport led each sovnarkoz to achieve as much independence of other regions as possible. "Regionalism" replaced "departmentalism" as the curse of the system.

In November 1962, Khrushchev announced another major organizational change. The 105 regional sovnarkozy were amalgamated into 47 new regional councils believed to be of more efficient scale. GOSPLAN's task was limited to long-term economic planning, and short-term production plans were formulated by the National Economic Council. Whatever their merits, the 1962 changes failed to resolve the basic flaws in the Soviet system of economic guidance. No doubt, this failure was a contributing factor to the replacement of Khrushchev by Kosygin in 1963.

Flaws in the Guidance System

Soviet experts agree that over-centralization of economic decision-making is a critical fault of their economy. Although it may have passed muster when the economy was smaller and simpler in structure, detailed central planning down to the enterprise level cannot cope with an economy with 2 million separate enterprises. Economic administration has become fantastically complex. Academician A. A. Dorodnitsyn stated that "in a growing economy the number of linkages and ties increases as the square of the number of separate elements, and the difficulty of plan optimization increases even faster—as the cube of the growing number of elements." V. M. Glushkov, a leading Soviet mathematician, calculated that the volume of economic planning and administration increases as the square of the gross product, and that if current methods were not changed, by 1980 the entire adult population of the U.S.S.R. would be employed in administration!

Marxist dogma has also been an impediment to Soviet officials in their search for better macromanagement of the economy and better micromanagement of enterprises. It obstructs rational allocation of capital among different uses by denying the legitimacy of interest and market prices. It deters provision of incentives by denying the informational value of profits. Soviet economists have displayed great ingenuity in inventing new labels for interest and profits. Their intellectual gymnastics in "modernizing" Leninist-Marxist theories have been amazing.

Soviet central planning today is essentially a pragmatic process, a compromise between ideology and reality. Plans for enterprises and industries are drawn up, based upon probably available labor, materials, equipment, transportation, and funds. These plans are reconciled by the National Economic Council. Defense, space, and "prestige" projects get top priority in claim on resources. Soviet writers refer to the process as "planning by material balances." It depends upon a rough input-output analysis of interindustry relationships, carried out primarily in physical terms but with value components as well.

The planning and control processes lead to numerous inefficiencies. The several elements of the Plan are not, in fact, coordinated. The central planners commonly over-commit basic commodities like steel, cement, or transport facilities. The result is a failure of timely delivery. A supply failure to one enterprise whose output is the raw material for another firm produces a chain reaction of delays. This contingency leads managers to accumulate heavy reserve stocks, and also to employ bribes and "special expediters" to obtain scarce raw materials or equipment. The stress put on fulfillment of physical output quotas leads enterprise managers to submit easily fulfilled quotas, or to produce goods of shoddy quality. Manpower needs are also commonly overstated. Costs and expense estimates are padded. Research and development expenses for new products and product improvements are minimized. From the point of view of the enterprise manager there is organizational confusion, uncertainty about his allotment of resources, and numerous *ad hoc* changes in plans to which adjustments must be made. The long chain of command generates mountainous paperwork, delays in decisions, and conflicts of authority. All of these flaws show up in the poor average quality of construction and commodities to be observed in the Soviet Union. Only the priority projects are well executed.

Kosygin's Reform Program

In September 1965, Premier Kosygin made an epochal address to the Central Committee of the Communist Party. It was a devastating criticism of Soviet economic planning and enterprise management. He outlined three proposals for reform: improvement of the planning process by explicitly incorporating provision for technological change; delegation of wider discretionary powers to enterprise managers and reduction of the number of central controls; motivation and measurement of the performance of enterprises through the use of profits, bonuses, markets, and credit. Kosygin also emphasized the need for a larger supply of competent managers with training in economics as distinguished from the traditional engineering background. He proposed the re-establishment of the industrial ministries abolished by Khrushchev in 1957; but he limited their task to staff supervision of industries and the administration of research and development institutes. He concluded his historic statement on a defensive note. Capitalist countries would say that the Soviet Union is turning to capitalist methods because socialist planning has failed. This is false. The essence of an economic system, he averred, is the ownership of the instruments of production, and the state will continue to own them in the U.S.S.R.

The central reform was to make the enterprise the basic building block of the Russian economy. Kosygin asigned an important decision-making role to its management. Henceforth, enterprise performance would be measured by sales rather than output, thus giving the firm incentive to satisfy its customers rather than merely seek to fulfill a quota assigned from above. Its efficiency was also to be gauged by an index of profitability that would reflect quality improvements and cost reductions as well as output. The amount of profits left in the enterprise by the state would be in direct proportion to its effective use of fixed assets (i.e., its rate of return), to the rate of increase in its sales, to the improvement in the quality of its products, and to the rise in its profits. Its capital investment would be financed in part by deductions from its profits ("retained earnings") and depreciation allowances, and in part by interest-bearing loans from the state. Formerly, capital outlays had been wholly financed by interest-free grants by the state, which did not lead to efficient use of capital. Bonuses were thereafter to be based upon enterprise profits rather than fulfillment of production quotas. Enterprises managed with exceptional efficiency would have more profits to pay higher bonuses and fringe benefits to their managements and workers. Part of profits was to be set aside to finance housing and social and cultural programs for employees.

Kosygin proposed abolition of the myriad of detailed goals and regulations heretofore straitjacketing enterprise managers. The following seven annual targets would be fixed by the central planners for each firm: volume of sales, product mix, maximum wage and salary payments, profit and profit rate, payments to the federal budget, amount of capital investment, and prices. Within these constraints, the individual manager would have plenary power to organize and operate his enterprise with the aim of maximizing its profit, and would have strong incentives to do so.

Kosygin's program was substantially accepted by the Communist Central Committee and by the Council of Ministers, which, on October 4, 1965, adopted the Statute on the Socialist State Production Enterprise, defining the rights of an enterprise and the authority of its management. Although it was too early to judge the results by mid-1966, the indications were favorable. Certainly, long steps were taken to rationalize enterprise management, and it would be natural to expect gains in efficiency.

The Kosygin program must be viewed only as a first step in a protracted process of reforming Soviet economic management. It was a tactical, not a strategic, change. Basic guidance continued to be provided by the State Plan, rather than by prices of goods and services impersonally determined in markets through the competition of enterprises for the favor of customers. Soviet prices continued to be set by the State Committee on Prices, by a process so involved as to defy description. They are supposed to be based upon *average* costs of production and to take market demand into account. In practice, they are fixed for each Five-Year Plan period, are subject only to officially approved revisions, and diverge widely from market realities. Soviet planners frankly admit that "the problem of price formation" is yet unresolved. Obviously, the *true* efficiency of an enterprise cannot be measured by its profits if both its raw material and finished product prices are fixed rigidly from above. Experts agree that present distortions in the Soviet price system are so great as to produce chaotic conditions, were market-determined prices to be introduced suddenly.

Prospects for 1966–1970

In 1966 the Communist Party Congress and the Council of Ministers approved a Five-Year Plan for 1966–1970. The official targets included a 7 per cent per year rise in the national income, a 4½ per cent annual rise in agricultural production, an 8½ per cent per year rise in industrial production, and a 6½ per cent annual rise in output per man-hour. The main thrusts of the new Plan were the modernization of plant and equipment, emphasis on agriculture, and a relative shift toward consumers' goods. Real income per person was scheduled to rise 30 per cent over the Plan period, implying a large increase in consumption.

Laggard Soviet agriculture, which left the country with the embarrassing need to make large foreign purchases of wheat during 1964–1965, received major attention in the 1966–1970 Plan. Agriculture's stock of fixed capital was to increase 90 per cent during the Plan period—a radical change from preceding Soviet policy. Prices of farm products were increased, and the annual delivery quotas stabilized. Bonus prizes were offered for above-quota deliveries. A minimum income was specified for workers on farms, and their credit facilities were improved. By all these measures it was hoped to raise output per man and per acre. The fact that nearly all of the increase in Soviet farm production since 1928 was achieved by expanding the area under cultivation testifies to past neglect of incentives to farmers and to overdependence upon nonintensive farming methods.

Despite repeated assurances of a better life, the Soviet consumer has remained low man on the planners' totem pole. Defense, space, heavy industry, and education have come first. These priorities were evident to the foreign visitor to Soviet cities in 1966. In Moscow he saw an impressive city of 6½ million people, built on a grand scale but mostly gray and grim and run down at the heel. The vast squares and boulevards held only light auto traffic. There was little color. Shops, service establishments and cafés were few and far between and of poor quality by Western standards. Advertising was almost totally absent.

Most people were rather shabbily dressed, and their demeanor was subdued. The contrast with the color, life, and gaiety of London, Paris, or West Berlin was striking. Life for the average Muscovite was hard, but no doubt better than in years past. A family was usually crowded with one or more others into an apartment whose kitchen and bathroom were shared. Recreational facilities were meager. There was little to relieve the discipline of daily toil.

The Soviet Government has been aware that consumers were restive. It understood, too, that consumer amenities are powerful incentives to continued effort. In recent years, it began to provide more of them. In 1966 the Soviet consumer could buy many durables on credit. He could purchase insurance. In theory, he could purchase a co-operative apartment in the city or a dacha in the country through long-term installment loans. Yet housing and durable goods were in very short supply, and waiting lists for deliveries were long.

Under the 1966–1970 Plan the Soviet consumer was promised a break. A 43–46 per cent rise was scheduled in the output of food and light industries, compared with a 36 per cent increase in the preceding five years. Waiting lists for durables were expected to dwindle, as the annual output of autos rose from 200,000 to 800,000, of refrigerators from 1,700,000 to 5,300,-000, of television receivers from 3,700,000 to 5,300,000. Ivan and Olga could hope for better food and clothing as enterprises were freed from petty tutelage and enabled to respond more flexibly to market demand. More protein foods, like meat and fish, were expected to displace some of the bread, potatoes, and sugars that have dominated the Russian diet.

Will the ambitious targets of the 1966–1970 Plan be attained? American experts on the Soviet economy doubt it. They point out that fulfillment of the Plan depends heavily upon an incredible rise in industrial and agricultural productivity. They assess the growth in Soviet GNP at no more than 4.5 per cent a year in the first half of the sixties. Only radical improvements in efficiency would boost the growth rate above this figure during the last half of the sixties, especially in view of the planned shift toward consumption and the relative decline in industrial investment. Barring large cutbacks in military and space outlays—which appear improbable—it is likely that the Soviet GNP will continue to rise in the range of 4 to 5 per cent a year. The gap between the national products of the United States and the U.S.S.R. will widen, not contract. Much will depend, however, upon the ability of the Soviet Government to improve its economic guidance system before 1970.

"Computoria" or the "Visible Hand"?

We may borrow Egon Neuberger's apt characterization of the two extreme schools of Soviet economic reform. The conservatives advocate "computoria"—a return to detailed central planning made more effective by mathematical methods and computers. The liberals, of whom Professor E. G. Liberman has been a leader, propose use of the "visible hand"—competition between state enterprises in markets to replace all except aggregative central planning. Which is likely to dominate Communist policy in the future?

Up to 1967 the Government was pursuing a middle course. It involved an increasing measure of enterprise independence and market guidance, along with a modernized and computerized central planning process. The Government planned to use 4,000 large computers by 1970 to facilitate the making of rational planning decisions and to eliminate the need for the millions of additional bureaucrats who would be necessary under previous planning methods.

Libermanism, or market socialism, has many advocates in the Soviet Union. Yet it poses a dilemma to Communist policymakers because it would require a radical change in the price structure. To be efficient, markets need an appropriate level of aggregate money demand, alternative sources for buyers, and flexible prices. These are lacking in the Soviet economy, and it will not be easy to create them. If all prices were suddenly freed from central dictation and allowed to find their natural levels in more or less competitive markets, a chaotic situation might ensue. During the transition from dictated to market prices, some enterprises would probably reap enormous profits and others would "go broke." Radical and quixotic changes might take place in the pattern of resource allocation. A gradual liberation of prices in several stages might avoid these consequences. Yet it would suffer from the grave political disadvantage of being opposed, at every stage, by bureaucrats with vested interests in the *status quo*. In the end, it might be preferable to risk disorganization through one wholesale reform of the pricing system than to suffer the agonies of "cutting off the puppy's tail by inches."

"Computoria" also has its own set of advantages and drawbacks in the eyes of Soviet policy-makers. On the plus side, it is likely that a wider usage of such sophisticated methods as mathematical model-building, input-output analysis, and linear programing, accompanied by massive use of computers, can improve the quality of state plans. Yet even Soviet mathematical economists are skeptical whether they can really solve the problem in an economy as huge and diverse as that of the Soviet Union. Difficult conceptual problems remain. How will anyone write the programs for the computers? The development of "software" will be infinitely more time-consuming than the building of the hardware.

The most tenable view in 1966 was that Communist policymakers would avoid radical changes, and that the U.S.S.R. was facing a prolonged period of experimentation with different systems of economic guidance. A pragmatic process of trial and error was likely to go on during the next decade. If this estimate proves correct, Soviet economic performance will continue to be hampered by many of the inefficiencies that plague it today. In the end, one may predict that market socialism will dominate the economy. If consumers are given freedom in spending their incomes, there is no appeal from the decision of the competitive market as to the optimal price to be placed upon any good or service.

Casting up the Balance Sheet

The Western observer can readily construct a list of both negative and positive factors regarding the achievements of Russian Communism after fifty years. On the negative side, one notes a regimented and joyless society, in which consumers' demands have been subordinated to industrial investment, military power, space exploration, and "prestige" projects. Despite its larger population and fully mobilized labor force, Soviet GNP is probably about half that of the United States. (Various experts using diverse methods put it between 40 to 60 per cent.) Per capita real income is no more than one third as high. The quality of consumer goods and of construction remains poor, although it has been improving. One observes great inefficiencies in the use of labor: everyone is employed but many inefficiently. He sees manifestly wasteful allocations of capital, including a misplaced emphasis upon such "prestige" projects in Moscow as the world's tallest radio and television tower and the world's largest hotel of 6,000 rooms. He discerns critical flaws in the economic guidance system that will require many years to correct.

On the other side of the ledger, the U.S.S.R. can point to positive accomplishments and impressive gains. The nation made a remarkably fast recovery from the devastation of World War II and the loss of 20 million citizens. Its dedication to popular education has produced universal literacy and scientific achievements second to none, as its sputniks and nuclear armament have shown. Soviet Russia's manpower (and womanpower) is mobilized to the practical limit, and there is no unemployment—for example, old women are used to sweep the streets with reed brooms! Indeed, it resembles the mobilization of the U.S. work force during World War II. An equally full utilization of American youth, women, and the elderly today would probably raise the GNP of the United States by 25 per cent or more! A comprehensive social-security system assures the Soviet citizen of protection against the main hazards of life, but its scale of benefits leaves the recipient within the current "poverty" classification of the United States. A wholesome attitude of egalitarianism pervades society. Those undertakings to which the central planners give priority get done, and done well. The physical planning of Russian cities, with their wide boulevards, parks, and absence of ugly billboard advertising, puts many American cities to shame.

The U.S.S.R. is a viable society, a going concern. The Russian people are living better than in the past, and hope for an even better future. Their economic and political freedoms can be expanded without fear of producing revolutionary changes. Their leaders are pragmatic but cautious in their search for greater economic efficiency. Yet, the Soviet economy is distinctly No. 2 in the world. The prospects are that it will remain in that position as far ahead as one is permitted to see.

Soviet-American Trade

In recent years trade between the two largest economies of the world has been miniscule. The United States exported only $23 million worth of goods to the U.S.S.R. during 1963 and imported only $21 million—hardly a ripple in the ocean of U.S. trade with the rest of the world, which involved $22 *billion* worth of merchandise exports. Indeed, American trade with all of the Eastern European Communist countries combined amounted to only $145 million of exports and $59 million of imports.

Soviet leaders are now eager to expand trade with the United States. They understand that the old Stalinist policy of complete economic autarchy runs counter to the U.S.S.R.'s real interests. They see in a larger interchange of goods opportunities to accelerate their technical progress. They desire primarily high-technology American products, such as computers, electronic systems, synthetic chemical and fiber plants, and advanced agricultural and industrial machinery, along with technical information and production know-how. Moreover, they are willing to liberalize their trading methods. Instead of confining trade to the bartering of specified goods, they propose that a wide variety of goods be bought by each country from the other, as circumstances make desirable. One Russian official said: "The U.S. and the U.S.S.R. have gotten out of the habit of trading with each other. They should begin to cultivate the trading habit again. The process should not start with a shopping list. Let us buy and sell whatever we each want."

Would U.S. interests be served by widening our trade with the Soviet Union? Should we reduce the list of goods now under embargo? These are much-debated issues, complicated by ideological and political differences.

One fact seems clear enough. The *economic* benefits of wider trade would be greater for the U.S.S.R. because Soviet demands for American goods are more urgent than American demands for commodities the Soviet Union is apparently able to supply. This is not, however, a valid argument against expanding trade. So long as both traders derive *some* benefit, trade enhances the welfare of both. It is also possible that wider exposure of American businessmen to Soviet products would reveal unsuspected opportunities. The notion that the U.S.S.R. has nothing that the United States wants, except gold, diamonds, vodka, furs, and caviar, may prove to be superficial. The allied idea that the United States will hold back Soviet economic progress by refusing to expand trade has little substance. West Germany, Britain, France, and other countries are conducting a thriving trade with the Soviet Union, which will grow to the degree that American trade does not.

Some argue that trade expansion with the U.S.S.R. carries the threat of increasing Communist propaganda and subversion. They say that Communists view trade as a political weapon in an ideological war rather than as a means of economic betterment. Today this danger is grossly exaggerated, if not quite illusory. Few Americans would consider exchanging their economic and political system for that of the Soviet Union. And no Soviet citizen would be permitted to advocate a capitalist system! The ideological warfare of the early postwar years has abated. Peaceful coexistence is the order of the day.

Indeed, the weight of the argument probably runs in the other direction. The United States may well derive larger *political* values from expanded trade than the U.S.S.R. Increasing trade inevitably would involve more travel and communication between Americans and Russians. It would bring a greater penetration of American ideas into the Soviet Union as well as of Soviet ideas into the United States. It could pave the way for a relaxation of East-West tensions and a lowering of the appalling burden of defense that both nations have been carrying. We should not forget that the United States has been the great exponent and practitioner of liberal international trade and investment policies in the world, despite occasional backsliding. Surely our economic and political strength is great enough to warrant progressive steps to extend trade with the Soviet Union. A policy of gradualism is best, with successive liberalization as confidence is gained. We should *separate* the issue of trade with the Soviet Union from that of trade with other European Communist countries, or with Communist China, or with Cuba. Different economic, political, and military considerations are involved in each case.

Selected Sources and References for Chapter 6

Committee for Economic Development, *East-West Trade; A Common Policy for the West.* Washington: May 1965.

Grossman, Gregory. "Innovation and Information in the Soviet Economy," *American Economic Review,* Vol. LVI, No. 2 (May 1966), p. 118.

Johnson, D. Gale. "The Environment for Technical Change in Soviet Agriculture," *American Economic Review*, Vol. LVI, No. 2 (May 1966), p. 145.

Joint Economic Committee of the U.S. Congress. *New Directions in the Soviet Economy*. Studies prepared for the Subcommittee on Foreign Economic Policy. Part I. Economic Policy; Part II. Economic Performance; Part III. The Human Resources; Part IV. The World Outside. Washington: U.S. Government Printing Office, 1966.

Kosygin, A. N. "On Improving Industrial Management, Perfecting Planning and Enhancing Economic Incentives in Industrial Production," *Problems of Economics*, Vol. VIII, No. 6 (October 1965).

Liberman, E. G.; Baibakov, N. K.; and Gatovskii, L. "Reform of Soviet Economic Management and Planning," *Problems of Economics*, Vol. VIII, No. 9 (January 1966).

Neuberger, Egon. "Libermanism, Computoria and Visible Hand," *American Economic Review*, Vol. LVI, No. 2 (May 1966), p. 131.

Nutter, G. Warren. *The Growth of Industrial Production in the Soviet Union*. Princeton: Princeton University Press, 1962.

Richman, Barry M. *Soviet Management with Significant American Comparisons*. New York: Prentice-Hall, 1965.

————. *Management Development and Education in the Soviet Union*. MSU International Business Studies. Michigan State University. East Lansing, Michigan, 1967.

Schwartz, Harry. *The Soviet Economy Since Stalin*. Philadelphia: J. B. Lippincott Company, 1965.

USSR: 1966. *Budget Plan and Foreign Policy*. Moscow: Novosti Press Agency Publishing House, 1966.

7. Prospects for Economic Growth: West and East

The U.S. Growth Gap of the Fifties

During the late 1950's Americans were dismayed by the contrast between the strong upsurge of production in both Western and Eastern Europe (with the notable exception of Britain) and the relatively slower growth of output in their own country. In 1958 most European countries could look back on a decade of steady 5–7 per cent yearly gains in their real GNP, while Americans were contemplating an average rise of only 3.3 per cent. These were the days when Khrushchev boasted that the Soviet Union would soon overtake and surpass the United States and that communism would bury capitalism. The Joint Economic Committee of the U.S. Congress held lengthy hearings and made studies of comparative economic growth. Tons of paper and ink were used

85

in playing a growth "numbers game." The outcome of these comparisons rather clearly favored Europe, both East and West of the Iron Curtain.

Professional economic journals and the press were filled with speculations about the reasons for the laggard performance of the U.S. economy. Western European observers scolded the United States for various sins of commission and omission in its economic policies. Communist ideologists had powerful ammunition to fire into the "uncommitted world" of Asian, African, and Latin American nations about the superiority of state central planning. Many Americans were apprehensive that the U.S. economy, while still incomparably larger than any other, was slipping. Would it be able indefinitely to support U.S. political and military commitments in the world and at the same time to improve living standards at home? These concerns were a factor in John F. Kennedy's election to the presidency in 1960, on a promise to "get the U.S. economy moving ahead."

What caused the slower economic growth rate of America during the fifties? No doubt its economic circumstances and policies both had a part. The United States was growing from a vastly larger base than European countries, and it had no "opportunities" to replace war-damaged plant with modern equipment. It could not borrow advanced technologies but had to push forward technological frontiers by its own efforts. It also bore a much heavier burden of defense which, during the Korean conflict of 1950–1953, absorbed up to 15 per cent of its GNP. Yet U.S. economic policies of the fifties were also culpable. Overly tight federal tax and spending policies in the last half of the decade created a "fiscal drag" on the economy. Growth-promoting changes in the revenue and expenditure structures of government were late in being adopted. And little progress was made in creating more pervasive competition, which led to an unfortunate "cost-push" on prices during 1956–1957.

Convergence of Growth, 1960–1965

Ironically, at the very time when America appeared to be losing the "growth game," the performance of the players began to change. As we have shown, the years around 1960 were marked by the beginnings of a slowdown in the economic progress of leading European countries, both West and East. This slowdown began at various dates in different countries, and it had divergent causes. Among the countries examined here, retardation first appeared in the Soviet Union about 1958, somewhat later in Poland, and around 1963 in France and West Germany. Only in Britain, where postwar progress had been consistently slow, was there a modest rise in the growth rate during the early 1960's.

Among the Western countries, the primary reasons for a change from fast to moderate growth were the emergence of limitations upon additional manpower, capital, and management, an exhaustion of easy technological opportunities to exploit, growing structural "bottlenecks," and recurrent wage and price inflation. These factors were also involved to some degree in the waning growth rates of the Russian and Polish economies. In addition, Communist countries had to confront the rising inefficiencies of central planning and weak incentives.

The economic performance of the U.S. economy during the first half of the sixties was a refreshing change to Americans. Sparked by large gains in manpower, rapid advances in technology arising from the "research revolution" since World War II, and growth-promoting changes in fiscal policy, the real output of the American economy rose 5.0 per cent a year during the period 1960–1966. This favorable turnabout was partly accounted for by substantial increments to the labor force and by the reduction of unemployment. More important was the rise in productivity in the private sector—from about 2.5 per cent a year during 1948–1958 to about 3.2 per cent a year during 1960–1966. Output per man-hour went up faster in the recent period because of better education and training of workers, higher investment in mechanization and automation, and improved management.

Economic policies also contributed to the good result. The "New Economics" provided for tax reductions and a federal budget designed to maintain demand at a full-employment level. Government offered accelerated depreciation and an investment credit to keep business investment high. Enlarged public outlays on highways, education, manpower retraining, and regional development raised productivity while reducing structural unemployment. Thus the U.S. economy was growing faster than most economies of Europe, reversing the previous postwar trends. No longer were Communists boasting of economic superiority nor were West Europeans complaining of U.S. policy blunders. The important question, however, was whether the new trends would continue, especially in view of U.S. inflation during 1966 and 1967. Will the U.S. economic growth rate during the next decade outstrip those of the major European countries, or will it revert to its postwar doldrums?

U.S. Growth in the Next Decade

History teaches the danger of generalizing from economic experience of five or ten years. Only in a long time perspective can valid comparisons be made of economic performance and its causes. Comparisons of the average annual growth rates in the real production of the United States and leading Western countries over very long periods of time have been developed by the National Institute of Economic and Social Research of London. For the United States and three of the countries surveyed in this volume, they show the following:

		AVERAGE ANNUAL RATES OF GROWTH TO 1960		
	Starting year of figures	Real product per man-year	Working age population	Total real national product
United States	1871	2.0	1.7	3.8
France	1855	1.5	0.1	1.6
Germany	1853	1.5	1.1	2.6
United Kingdom	1857	1.2	0.7	2.0

Evidently, the long-term growth rate of the U.S. economy has been high. This is because of *both* a more rapid rise in the labor force and a substantially larger annual gain in productivity. (Unfortunately, lack of data prevents one from making similar comparisons with the leading Communist countries.) The figures warrant a conclusion that faster American growth in the future would be in character with our past. The relatively good performance of the early sixties is not an aberration from the "normal" relationship with Western Europe.

The figures also dramatize the two crucial determinants of economic growth: work force and productivity—or, more precisely, man-hours worked in an economy and output per man-hour. During the period 1871–1960, the increase in the U.S. population of working age, fed by heavy immigration up to 1920 and by larger participation of women, played nearly as important a role in U.S. economic growth as did gains in productivity. Since World War II, annual gains in productivity have been the increasingly dominant cause of growth, although the annual rate of increase in the work force has continued with natural population increase and the rising participation of women.

A careful estimate of the potential growth of the U.S. economy over the period 1960–1975 was made in 1960 by James W. Knowles for the Joint Economic Committee of Congress. Knowles concluded that an average annual gain in real output of 4.2 per cent a year was reasonable. Although this is short of the actual gain of 5.0 per cent made during 1960–1966, the Knowles figure is a measure of *potential growth at full employment,* and some part of the rise in output during 1960–1966 was attributable to taking up slack in the economy. Even so, one may argue that Knowles's estimate is probably on the low side. In the first place, it assumes *no* material change in present U.S. structural policies. Secondly, it probably understates future annual average gains in productivity.

There are many changes that the U.S. Government could make in its economic policies that would collectively promote growth by a significant factor. Even if we ignore policy changes that would be "costly" by requiring more work or less consumption from people, such "costless" changes as reductions of trade barriers, subsidies, price-fixing, or racial and sexual discrimination could, according to Edward Denison, add something like half a percentage point to the potential growth rate. This would bring it to an average of 4.7 per cent a year. In a 1966 up-dating of his earlier study, Knowles raised his estimate of potential growth to as much as 4.5 per cent a year during 1965–1975.

Apart from the rationalization of structural economic policies, it seems likely that the average annual gain in productivity will continue to rise in the future, as a consequence of booming expenditures on scientific research and development. Ever since World War II, R and D outlays have been rising about 15 per cent a year—more than three times the growth rate of the GNP. It appears that productivity gains react to R and D outlays after a time lag of several years. The upturn in the U.S. growth rate during 1960–1966 was due, in part, to the expansion of R and D outlays during the fifties. If so, we may expect larger annual productivity gains during the period 1966–1975 from the even larger R and D outlays made during 1960–1966.

Taking everything into account, average annual rises of 1.5 per cent in working population and of 3.0 per cent in labor productivity should make growth in the real product of the U.S. economy of 4.5 per cent during 1966–1975 quite probable. This assumes a prolongation of full-employment budgets, growth-promoting changes in the federal tax and expenditure systems, and success in preventing price inflation. Indeed, 5 per cent annual growth is attainable, if the American people make it a high-priority goal.

Future Western European Growth

A sustained high growth rate for the U.S. economy in the next decade is likely to stand in contrast with lower growth rates in France and West Germany. For reasons described in Chapters 3 and 4, the French and West German economies will have less rapid expansions of their working populations than in the recent past, and they will not be able to repeat the exceptionally large annual productivity gains made during 1950–1965. While figures on national production abound and international comparisons are tricky, the U.S. Agency for International Development has published data that are satisfactory for comparisons. A.I.D. puts the average annual growth rate of GNP during the five-year period 1960–1965 at 4.8 per cent for France and 4.7 per cent for West Germany. In that period, increases of about 1.5 per cent a year in working population were accompanied by gains in output per head of about 3.3 per cent a year. During the decade 1966–1975, one may expect a drop in the average annual increment to the working populations of these countries to under 1 per cent, and in GNP per head to about 3 per cent, notwithstanding gains from further economic integration of the E.E.C. An annual average growth of 4 per cent in GNP is probable. This is a less optimistic forecast than those of most Continental economists and planners, who are inclined to project past experience into the future. Yet it appears realistic in view of the tough structural problems and constraints on future progress which European economies confront.

In contrast to the leading Continental countries, the growth rate of the British economy is expected to make a moderate improvement over its tortoiselike past. A.I.D. figures show that British growth, which averaged 2.7 per cent a year during the fifties, rose to about 3.3 per cent a year during 1960–1965. We foresee an average annual gain of about 3.5 per cent in Britain's GNP during 1966–1975. This is somewhat less than the 3.8 per cent assumed by the National Institute of Economic and Social Research in its study *The British Economy in 1975*. Yet the Institute's estimate of a 3.5 per cent annual gain in output per worker appears over-optimistic in the light of a trend rate that was little over 2.3 per cent since World War II. Even to reach growth of 3.5 per cent a year implies strong growth-promoting changes in British economic policies. It also assumes that future British participation in the Common Market will help to enhance the competitive strength of its industry.

Future Eastern European Growth

The slower growth of the Soviet Union and Poland during 1960–1965 in comparison with the earlier postwar era has been explained in Chapters 5 and 6. We may expect the economic progress of these countries to continue at a moderate pace during 1966–1975. They, too, will be confronting smaller accessions of workers into their labor forces as a result of the World War II "baby gap," capital shortages, and exhaustion of traditional technologies. In addition, they face serious problems in efforts to improve the efficiency of labor, capital, and management. It will not be easy to graft concepts and practices of competitive enterprise onto their centrally planned and directed economic structures. Although these countries possess large pools of workers who are relatively unproductively employed in agriculture, the movement of these workers into more productive employment in other sectors will require much time and vast amounts of capital.

Foreign specialists on the Soviet economy believe that its GNP grew about 4.5 per cent a year during 1960–1965. It is unlikely to grow any faster during the decade 1966–1975. Indeed, strong efforts to reform and rationalize Soviet economic management will be necessary to keep the growth rate from falling below this level. Communist-bloc countries have not made much progress toward economic integration, and are unlikely to do so in the future. Thus, they will be deprived of the growth-promoting effects of closer integration that will be realized by the Western European countries through the E.E.C.

Implications of Converging Growth Rates

The first half of the sixties was marked by a convergence in the growth rates of the six economies included in this study. The fast-growth economies of Europe slowed up, while the slow-growth economies of the United States and the United Kingdom accelerated. The prospect is that these trends will continue, and that the real gross products of *all* these countries will grow within a narrow range of 3.5 to 4.5 per cent a year during the next decade. What are the implications of this recent and prospective convergence?

One clear implication is that the relative economic and political position of the United States in the world will be strengthened. As a fast-growing country, America will offer investment opportunities—to Europeans as well as Americans—that are expanding faster than those abroad. The large net outflow of U.S. investment capital to Europe should taper off, and it might even be reversed. The U.S. balance of international payments should improve, and the dollar should recover its early postwar position of strength.

Its stronger economic position should enable the United States to play an even more constructive and influential political role in the world. National security requirements would be less burdensome. Foreign economic assistance could be enlarged without cramping domestic programs. Above all, the example of a free economy that is already the world's richest maintaining a high rate of economic progress should have profound psychological and political effects upon all peoples. It should influence their choices of economic goals and policies.

A convergence of the British and Continental growth rates should make it easier for Britain to enter the Common Market. It is easier to harmonize the economic policies of nations that are progressing *pari passu*. With a British economy expanding nearly as rapidly as those of the largest Continental countries, the argument that Britain would be a drag on the E.E.C. would lose its force.

Convergence of the American and Soviet growth rates would also have interesting consequences. It should mute the ideological conflict over the relative merit of different social and economic systems. At the same time, international debate on economic policies could, hopefully, be rechanneled into more pragmatic and constructive themes. For example, the new environment might permit of wider international co-operation in solving the vast problem of engendering progress in the poor regions of the world.

PAST AND PROBABLE FUTURE GROWTH RATES OF LEADING ECONOMIES

	AVERAGE ANNUAL PERCENTAGE CHANGES			
	1950–55	*1955–60*	*1960–65*	*Probable 1966–75*
France				
GNP	4.1	5.0	4.8	4.0
Population	0.8	1.0	1.5	1.0
GNP per Head	3.3	4.0	3.3	3.0
West Germany				
GNP	9.5	6.3	4.7	4.0
Population	0.9	1.1	1.3	1.0
GNP per Head	8.6	5.2	3.4	3.0
United Kingdom				
GNP	2.7	2.8	3.3	3.5
Population	0.2	0.5	0.8	0.5
GNP per Head	2.5	2.3	2.5	3.0
United States				
GNP	4.3	2.2	4.5	4.5
Population	1.7	1.7	1.5	1.5
GNP per Head	2.6	0.5	3.0	3.0
Soviet Union				
National Income	7.0	6.0	4.5	4.5
Population	1.0	1.0	1.1	1.2
NI per Head	6.0	5.0	3.3	3.3
Poland				
National Income	8.6	6.6	5.5	4.5
Population	2.1	1.9	1.1	1.5
NI per Head	6.5	4.7	4.4	3.0

Estimates for 1950–1965 for all countries except Poland and the Soviet Union are by the U.S. Agency for International Development. All other estimates are by the authors.

Of course, the opening up of a positive "growth gap" between the United States and Western Europe could also raise new problems or revive old ones. The U.S. government may need to give more attention to ways of speeding the international trans- mission of advanced technologies. It may need to participate more actively in the improvement of management science and education. It may face claims that Uncle Sam should assume a larger share of free world defense burdens, of the United Na- tions, and of the development of economically backward re- gions. Yet, U.S. problems as a fast-growth country will certainly be less onerous than those it would face as a slow-growth country!

Selected Sources and References for Chapter 7

Beckerman, Wilfred. (ed.). *The British Economy in 1975.* Cam- bridge: Cambridge University Press, 1966.

Denison, Edward. *The Sources of U.S. Economic Growth and the Choices before Us.* New York: Committee for Economic Develop- ment, 1962.

"Economic Growth: The Last One Hundred Years," in *National In- stitute Economic Review,* No. 16 (July 1961). London.

Geary, R. C. (ed.). *Europe's Future in Figures.* Vol. 1. Amsterdam: North-Holland Publishing Company, 1962.

Knowles, James W. *The Potential Economic Growth in the United States.* Study Paper No. 20 in Study of Employment, Growth and Price Levels for the Joint Economic Committee of Congress. Washington: U.S. Government Printing Office, 1960.

————. *U.S. Economic Growth to 1975: Potentials and Problems.* Study prepared for the Joint Economic Committee of Congress. Washington: U.S. Government Printing Office, 1966.

Lecht, Leonard A. *Goals, Priorities and Dollars: The Next Decade.* New York: The Free Press, 1966.

Maddison, Angus. *Economic Growth in the West.* New York: The Twentieth Century Fund, 1964.

8. Convergence of Economic Guidance Systems

Our studies of six advanced economies in the mid-sixties have revealed evidence in favor of the "convergence hypothesis"—the idea that the economic guidance systems of governments in both Eastern and Western European countries are becoming similar. The important questions are whether convergence is real or illusory, whether it will continue, and what its implications are for the industrially developed world.

There are two opposing views of the structures and dynamics of the economies of the East—such as the U.S.S.R. and Poland—and those of the West—notably France, Britain, West Germany, and the United States. The first view is that, despite numerous and even profound differences, all of these economies are *essentially* similar. The alternative view, of course, is that, notwithstanding many and even important similarities, the economies of East and West are essentially unlike.

These contrasting views are often stated in dynamic terms. Protagonists of the view that similarities outweigh dissimilarities ordinarily maintain that the economies of the East and West are converging through time. The convergionists are naturally opposed by the separatists, who see the East and West diverging, or at least continuing in different paths. This fascinating issue of convergence of East and West is not limited to economics. It carries over into political science, sociology, and even national defense. But economics is the usual arena of discussion, and a trend toward convergence of economics systems is the popular view.

The tourist traveling through the great cities of eastern and western Europe during the sixties certainly would share this popular view. Soviet, German, and British cities, for example, are growing with soaring skyscrapers that would be at home in New York. Consumer goods in the shops of France, Poland, and the United States are often indistinguishable at first glance. And so on. But the social scientist must probe beyond superficial appearances. He must observe and compare economic goals and problems, institutions and actions, methods and systems. Only then can he venture on opinion.

Convergionists versus Separatists

Convergionists point to greater acceptance in the East of incentive wages, decentralized decision-making, economic calculations such as marginalism and mathematical programming, and imputed cost-of-capital. In the West they see more government planning, wage and price controls, social goods, and governmental ownership of enterprises. From these changes in economic institutions and methods they conclude that convergence is dominant, and that, as Toynbee predicted, "It will only be a matter of time before there will be little to choose between America and Russia."

The anticonvergionists are quick, however, to cite continuing economic differences that support their position. They point to the bipolar attitudes toward private property in East and West, asserting that this alone will prevent convergence. Yet citizens of Communist countries have gradually acquired the right to own their houses and a widening range of personal property. They note different goals and problems: growth versus moderating fluctuations, capital versus consumer goods, or excess demand versus excess supply. They argue that the East (especially the U.S.S.R.) has been and will be characterized by the pressure of unfilled demand upon scarce resources, whereas the opposite problem is endemic in the West (especially the United States). The chronic sellers' market in the East and the chronic buyers' market in the West are said to be so shaping economic institutions in the two groups of economies that convergence becomes less likely every day. However, the recent emergence of local consumer-goods surpluses in the U.S.S.R. and of inflation and shortages of goods in the United States casts doubt on this argument. Perhaps the East is moving partially to conditions of overproduction, while the West is moving the other way, toward underproduction!

At a fundamental level, the controversy centers on the effectiveness and viability of "capitalistic" versus "communistic" institutions. Here one would expect major social changes if existing institutions were ineffective, but only minor changes otherwise. Thus, the convergionists would argue that Western economic management has moved and will continue to move "leftward" in order to meet more effectively contemporary problems of instability, inequality, monopoly, and so on. For the East, they cite the well-known difficulties the Soviets are having with doctrinaire central planning in the face of a maturing, complex economy.

One need only look at the *modifications* of Western capitalism in recent times to see that it has proved itself capable of adapting to and meeting new challenges. Better macromanagement of national economies, more comprehensive social-security programs, modification of extremes in the behavior of the private sector, and longer-run planning horizons in making public and private decisions are all cases in point. Need for further movement "to the left" may be unnecessary in the future. Similarly, the remarkable strength and vitality of Soviet Communism may enable it to modify and improve its institutions and processes to meet new problems without a *major* shift "rightward."

Competitive Market Pricing and Private Enterprise

To an economist, however, there is one test of convergence of economic systems which transcends all others. This is the role of the competitive market in determining prices. If consumer wants and preferences are permitted, through the market place, to direct the allocation of resources into alternative uses, then we have an economic system that is *fundamentally* different from a system in which the allocation of resources is governed by the preferences and values of state central planners. The market economy may be severely modified by monopoly, government controls, and public enterprises; but it is still significantly different from the state-planned economy, even though the latter may have some of the trappings of markets.

The signals or indicators of the market economy are market prices. Prices carry *information* from millions of consumers to enterprises which, in turn, relay it to factor owners (including labor). This information not only enables but compels resource adjustments to satisfy consumers. If, as in most Eastern economies, prices are more or less arbitrarily fixed by the planners, then the market is not being used to transmit valuable information to enterprise managers and factor owners.

Judged by the criterion of the role of competitive market prices, we can say that there is evidence that the East is moving toward the West—but not vice versa. Indeed, the West is continuing to extend and to improve the market pricing system (i.e., the European Common Market). The hard imperatives of efficiency are compelling the socialist countries to turn increasingly to competitive market pricing and to profitability as a measure of economic performance. But will they continue to introduce "market socialism"? Are recent changes permanent, or will the next shift in political power lead to a regression? Although the evidence is inconclusive and the outcome is yet in doubt, we believe that the prospect in the mid-sixties is one of continuing convergence by the East.

The West is making other significant institutional changes which give an appearance of convergence by it as well. Western countries are finding that their economic performance is improved by the introduction of long-term planning, especially by tying government budgets to such plans. Modern complex economies seem to require market guidance; but market guidance alone generates results deemed inadequate in today's world.

There is another important gauge of convergence in economic systems: the changes in the relative roles of private and of state enterprise. Here, again, there is evidence of some movement of the East toward the West, particularly in agriculture, but not of the West toward the East. Both Russia and Poland enlarged the shares of private farm production and of small private trade and service firms in recent years. In the Western economies, one notes the privatization of a few large industrial enterprises in West Germany and the renationalization of the steel industry in Britain, but no significant trend. The *basic* commitments of the East to state enterprise and of the West to private enterprise appear to be as strong as ever.

To point to a degree of convergence in economic policies between West and East, is not, of course, to forecast an ultimate reconciliation and integration of governmental economic guidance. Such an event is most improbable, given the wide gap that separates the economic ideologies. Not in our lifetime is the Soviet Union likely to be "the same" as the United States, nor Poland "the same" as West Germany.

Implications of Convergence

Nevertheless, there are interesting and hopeful implications of the degree of convergence of economic policies that has ocurred and will occur. As the advanced nations come to see that the solutions to their economic problems require less dissimilar policies, the sharpness and acrimony of the debate over economic ideology will surely diminish. A more promising groundwork will be laid for relaxation of political tensions. The probability will rise of more common approaches to world problems.

It is becoming clear that the most intractable economic problems are not those of the advanced countries but those that confront the underdeveloped world. It is in dealing with the problems of elevating additional societies into the ranks of modern industrialized nations that the hardest problems, and the most fierce debates about policies to solve them, will emerge in the future. What is the proper role of the government in an underdeveloped country? What is the optimum role for private enterprise? How can government and private enterprise be harnessed into an effective team for rapid development? These are issues that go beyond the purview of this book. Yet they are likely to emerge as the dominant economic issues of the future, just as the issues of socialistic versus capitalistic policies recede in the advanced countries.

Selected Sources and References for Chapter 8

Bergson, Abram; Chamberlin, Neil; and Tangri, Shanti S. "The Convergence Hypothesis: Planning and Market Elements in the Development of Soviet, Western and Developing Countries," *American Economic Review*, May 1967.

Deutscher, Isaac. *The Great Contest, Russia and the West*. New York: Oxford University Press, 1960.

Shonfield, Andrew. *Modern Capitalism*. London: Oxford University Press, 1965.

Turgeon, Lynn. *The Contrasting Economies*. Boston: Allyn and Bacon, Inc., 1963.

Wellisz, Stanislaw. *The Economies of the Soviet Bloc*. New York: McGraw-Hill Book Company, 1964.

9. Lessons for the United States

Since World War II America has exported much economic and business knowledge to Europe. West Europeans are the first to concede this fact when they point, often in tones of apprehension, to the "Americanization" of their continent. They fear that their own national ideologies and ways of life will be blurred, if not swallowed up. American economic ideas, business practices, living standards, social habits, and even language have followed U.S. capital, management, and enterprise to all corners of Western Europe. Mass markets for consumer goods have developed. Retail distribution has undergone a revolution. Competition has been energized, advertising and sales promotional efforts have burgeoned. Mass ownership of radio and television sets, household appliances, and automobiles have given millions of people a new freedom and mobility. Rising wages and living standards have accompanied the mechanization of industry to serve mass markets. While postwar Europe would have produced many economic changes on its own, there can be no doubt that America was the prototype, provided leadership, and greatly accelerated the pace of European change. The United States has run a large surplus in its balance of trade in economic and business knowledge.

Europe can also teach the United States valuable economic lessons. Americans would be wise to study ways in which European countries have sought to deal with problems common to all advanced economies. Larger imports of economic knowledge could advance American welfare, while balancing Europe's accounts in this invisible item of trade. Whether it involves knowledge or commodities, international trade must ultimately run two ways if it is to endure. Lessons may be learned from European experience in dealing with U.S. economic tasks such as long-term fiscal planning and budgeting, long-term planning of physical environments, combatting regional stagnation, reducing structural unemployment, restraining price inflation, and eliminating continental trade barriers. Obviously, this is an incomplete list of subjects and is intended to be illustrative. Some European experiences with these problems are negative and teach what not to do; others are positive and offer prototypes for emulation by the United States.

Long-term Fiscal Planning and Budgeting

Americans can learn from Europeans—particularly East Europeans—the values of long-term planning of governmental budgets and economic policies. While no informed American would espouse Soviet-style central planning and control of the whole economy, he should nevertheless recognize the important values of a five-year advance look at the probable course of U.S. fiscal policy and governmental finances.

By law the U.S. President presents to Congress each January an *annual* budget of the federal government which, including the federal trust funds, sets forth a plan for raising and spending about 20 per cent of the nation's income. The federal budget has such enormous influence upon the behavior of the economy that it is a tool for its management; and it should be designed to facilitate the making of rational decisions regarding the best allocations of governmental burdens and resources. Nearly all important revenue and expenditure programs last more than one year, and decisions made each year depend primarily upon decisions made in preceding years. Being limited to comparisons of income and outlays in a single year, the present budget does not provide Congress with a good basis for action.

Congress should know the *future* budget commitments to ongoing spending programs—such as space, weapon systems, or highways—that are implied by the current year's expenditures. It should be able to compare the social returns from alternative programs to attain the same objective (e.g., aid to worker retraining and relocation versus subsidies for industrial relocation and area development). It should be able to judge the costs and benefits of different annual rates of spending on a program (e.g., a 25-year national highway program versus a 15-year program). In short, it needs "program" budgets. While all spending programs should be annually reviewed and, if necessary, revised, each federal budget should show prospective outlays on each program five years in advance, along with five-year revenue plans to finance them. Thus, current fiscal decisions could be made in the light of their future implications, yielding a more productive use of federal resources. These principles are equally applicable to the budgeting and fiscal policies of our state and local governments

An important by-product of advance fiscal planning would be *fiscal principles* to guide budget actions. For example, the heavy reliance of the federal revenue system upon progressive income taxes results, with normal economic growth, in the "automatic" generation of about $7 billion of additional revenue each year at constant tax rates. Congress should adopt a long-term plan for the disposition of these revenues, involving either reduction of tax rates, expansion of federal expenditures, revenue-sharing with the states, or a combination of these measures. Of course, such a fiscal plan should take into account the overriding need to use the federal budget as an instrument to stabilize the U.S. economy at full employment—with deficits when there is unemployment and surpluses when there is over-employment.

American governments have been laggard in adopting long-term budgeting and fiscal planning, although their use has become common among U.S. business corporations. Among the federal agencies, long-term program budgeting was first utilized in the Department of Defense. A breakthrough occurred in August 1965, when President Johnson called upon the heads of all federal agencies to introduce the program planning and budgeting system (PPBS). It is hoped that planning in each federal agency will rapidly advance to the point where an integrated five-year federal budget can be presented annually to Congress. With similar action by state and local governments, the resulting improvement in the quality of public revenue and spending decisions could add significantly to U.S. economic growth.

Environmental Planning

The physical environments for living and working in many American cities are now unsatisfactory and, in some, intolerable. They contrast unfavorably with the environments of such European cities as London, Paris, or Milan. Air and water pollution, congested auto traffic, poor mass-transit facilities, over-intensive and helter-skelter building, want of parks and recreational space, and ugly billboard advertising and above-ground utility poles have been the product of years of neglect of long-term planning of American cities. Yet there is no escape from planning. Even no plan *is* a plan—a bad one! Few Americans, returning home from a European tour, fail to wonder why citizens of the richest nation on earth do not have *all* of the conveniences, amenities, and aesthetic satisfactions enjoyed by the Londoner or the Parisian. (Of course, America does excel in providing *some* of them.)

Europeans—both East and West—have much to teach the United States about environmental planning and development. While the automobile has brought new problems to Europe's cities, their centuries of experience in planning the construction and rebuilding of urban areas can help us complete a major task on the American agenda. Lacking empty western lands to move to, Europeans have long since had to come to terms with their environment.

One major U.S. need is a better integration of physical planning activities. There is poor co-ordination of the activities of municipalities, regions, states, and the federal government, and of *physical and fiscal* planning. Integration of U.S. local governments on a metropolitan basis is an essential condition of progress. Our sprawling metropolises are now governed by an over-lapping patchwork of local authorities designed for the horse-and-buggy era, with authority and responsibility carved up into small pieces.

Another condition of progress is long-term commitment to plans by governments that have the resources as well as the power to carry them out. The poverty of U.S. local governments, with their heavy responsibilities, contrasts sharply with the affluence of the federal government. The comparative simplicity of European governmental organization, with its greater centralization of authority and financial ability, has been a factor in its success. In Eastern Europe, of course, the machinery for physical planning is integrated with that for general economic planning. As a result, the physical features of some Soviet cities, for example, with their tree-lined boulevards, parkways, and squares, put many American cities to shame.

Metropolitan areas must be seen as co-ordinated *systems* of residential, business, transportation, recreational, and educational facilities, for which the goals are to optimize the quality of living as well as economic efficiency. U.S. businesses have developed the "systems approach" to the development of such complex products as the Polaris missile. Surely, U.S. governments can apply this concept to the improvement of our cities.

Combatting Regional Stagnation

As the U.S. economy has grown, certain regions, like Appalachia, have been left behind in the economic race. Even when national employment is high and the stream of prosperity is flowing full, there are stagnant pools of chronic unemployment and low incomes. Apart from the Tennessee Valley, whose industrial progress was greatly stimulated by TVA, the U.S. government has had comparatively little experience in designing and managing programs of development for chronically backward and depressed areas. In contrast, European countries have had a rich experience in this field. The Soviet Union has, over the years, planned and developed whole cities and regions in previously unindustrialized provinces of its vast land.

Foreign regional development should be more extensively studied by the U.S. government for the lessons it teaches—both positive and negative. British efforts to redevelop northeast

England, Scotland, and South Wales appear so far to have met with only qualified success. Government agencies have offered grants, "soft" loans, and generous leases on newly built factories to entice industries to areas of persistently large unemployment. Although not without effect, British regional development policies have nevertheless not prevented an increasing concentration of industry in the Midlands and around London.

Development of backward regions by various forms of public subsidy is only one way to utilize their unemployed labor. The other way is to provide public aids to the retraining and relocation of their manpower in areas where jobs exist. There are pros and cons to each policy, and no doubt both should be employed. Beyond a certain point, however, they compete for public funds, and decisions must be made as to where the margin of substitution lies. In a market-oriented economy, whose government would never *order* either a man or a factory to move, except in a national emergency, financial inducements must be offered to get voluntary action.

Reducing Structural Unemployment

Structural unemployment—the mismatch between the skills of unemployed workers and those demanded by enterprises having vacant jobs—is an important American economic problem. President Kennedy admitted this when, in his 1962 *Economic Report,* he proposed to accept a 4 per cent unemployment ratio (i.e., 96 per cent of the labor force employed) as an "interim" definition of "full employment" in the U.S. economy. Four per cent is more than twice the reported average unemployment rate in advanced Western European countries during the past decade. (Communist countries deny the existence of *any* unemployment, asserting that those not at work are "in process of selecting jobs.") The relatively high U.S. ratio of structural unemployment has many causes. The large area of our economy, its affluence, the high mobility of people, the presence of large minority groups, and the "soft" method used by the U.S. Department of Labor in measuring unemployment—all play a part. Most significant is the fact that the U.S. economy is technologically dynamic and vigorously competitive.

The progressive mechanization and automation of trade and service as well as of manufacturing industries will increase the amount of structural unemployment in the United States, unless workers displaced from conventional tasks are retrained for new ones and youths are fitted by education and training for the jobs of the future. To reduce the ratio of structural unemployment will require more vigorous efforts than have been made so far.

Western European countries have had long experience in dealing with structural unemployment, even though they, too, will have more of it in the future. Their experiences range over a broad field, including apprenticeship and vocational education, worker retraining, relocation grants and loans, and provision of housing in expanding areas. An active international interchange of knowledge could help all Western countries increase their employment ratios and add to their growth.

Restraining Price Inflation

Western European countries have long shared with the United States the problem of restraining price inflation. In some countries the problem has been continuous; in others, sporadic. In some, the primary cause has been the upward pull of excessive demand; in others, the upward push of rising wage rates. Some have maintained the buying power of their monetary unit better than others; none has succeeded in stabilizing the price level, although the United States has come closest to this goal.

Two behavioral characteristics of the Western economies lie at the root of price inflation. The first is the tendency of public spending for welfare, defense, and infra-structure to outrun public revenues, leading to deficits and an excessive aggregate demand for goods and services. The second is the tendency of labor unions to press for, and to obtain, wage increases that are larger than gains in labor productivity, leading to higher costs. Of course, the two causes are interrelated. Booming governmental expenditures help to produce tight labor markets in which unions can obtain excessively large wage increases.

Western European countries have sought to restrain price inflation by monetary restraints upon the growth of aggregate demand, and by adopting "incomes policies" aimed at holding annual wage increases (as well as increases in the incomes of other economic groups) down to annual gains in productivity. As noted previously, these policies have not attained their purpose. Although European monetary policies were restrictive most of the time, fiscal policies contributed to the expansion of aggregate demand, especially during the early sixties. Major reliance therefore was placed, both in Britain and on the Continent, upon "incomes policies" to limit wage increases. Careful assessment of their operation by European and American economists has produced a consensus that their effects were very limited in extent and duration. While they sometimes suppressed wage and price increases temporarily, underlying pressures soon expressed themselves.

A most important lesson is that there is no substitute for governmental fiscal restraint—curbs on public spending, adequate tax rates, and budget surpluses—as a supplement to monetary restraint, if price inflation is to be curbed. Another lesson is that informal, "voluntary" procedures to hold wage increases within the bounds of productivity gains—*vide* the U.S. wage and price "guideposts"—is a weak and even mischievous instrument for preventing inflation. The power of labor unions to obtain excessive wage increases can only be curbed effectively in two ways: keeping aggregate demand down to a full-employment level, and creating adequate competition—foreign and domestic—in the markets of each country.

Neither Western European experience with "incomes policies" nor our own frustrating experience with "guideposts" encourage the United States to follow this path of economic policy. "Incomes" policies in the United States would be even less successful than they have been in Europe. Our economy is less dependent upon foreign trade and foreign competition. The social idea of "fair" income shares commands less support in America. And our economy is much larger with a more decentralized organization of labor and collective bargaining. The basic point, however, is that in a market-directed economy no economic group is entitled, by right, to a fixed share of the real national income. If an economy is to be efficient, income shares must vary over time, in accordance with changes in the supply-demand relationships of the factors of production. Competition is the best regulator of wages and prices.

Eliminating Continental Trade Barriers

The experience of the E.E.C. in eliminating internal barriers to trade among six nations and creating a common market provides the United States with a valuable laboratory for economic policy. If, as appears probable, Britain and the E.F.T.A. countries enter the E.E.C. during the late sixties, Western Europe would then constitute a unified continental market containing more than 300 million people. Western Europe would have forged ahead of North America. The American common market would embrace only the 200 million people of the fifty American states, and would fail to include the 70 million people of Canada and Mexico.

It is sometimes carelessly said that, in creating its common market, Europe merely caught up with the United States, because we have enjoyed the advantages of a continental market ever since a federal union of American states was completed from the Atlantic to the Pacific oceans in the mid-nineteenth century. This understates the real achievement of the E.E.C., which was to eliminate international trade barriers. To create free trade between sovereign nations is a much more formidable task than to create it between states in a federal union.

North Americans would be wise to consider how Western Europeans brought off their great achievement. Beyond doubt, free trade throughout North America would lead to greater efficiency in the use of resources and would foster the growth of all countries. Among basic ideas embodied in the Treaty of Rome were a gradual scaling-down of *internal* quotas and tariffs according to an agreed schedule over a twelve-year period; payment, on a diminishing scale, of subsidies and retraining and relocation allowances to industries and workers seriously injured by the liberalization of trade; and gradual movement over a twelve-year period to a uniform *external* tariff schedule between the E.E.C. and the rest of the world. The essence of the process was prior agreement on successive annual steps toward defined goals, as well as measures to ease adjustments during the transition.

The key ideas in the successful evolution of the E.E.C.—goals, gradualism, and adjustment—can be usefully applied to the development of a North American common market or, indeed, to common markets in other regions of the world, such as Central America, Latin America, or Pacific Asia. The E.E.C. has taught the world that the benefits of regional free trade can be realized without impairing national identities or obliterating political differences. Whether or not the E.E.C. will take steps toward political as well as economic integration is a moot question. Even if it does not do so, it will stand as a model of enlightened economic statesmanship for emulation by the world.

Selected Sources and References for Chapter 9

Area Redevelopment Policies in Britain and the Countries of the Common Market. Area Redevelopment Administration, U.S. Department of Commerce. Washington: U.S. Government Printing Office, 1965.

Governmental Policies to Deal with Prices in Key Industries in Selected Foreign Countries. Paper No. 2 of Economic Policies and Practices. Materials Prepared for the Joint Economic Committee of Congress. Washington: U.S. Government Printing Office, 1963.

Klaassen, Leo H. *Area Social and Economic Development.* Paris: Organization for Economic Cooperation and Development, 1966.

Meany, George L.; Blough, Roger; and Jacoby, Neil H. *Government Wage-Price Guideposts in the American Economy.* Moscowitz Lectures in Public Policy. New York: New York University Press, 1967.

Modernizing Local Government. A Statement by the Research and Policy Committee of the Committee for Economic Development. New York: July 1966.

Novick, David. (ed.). *Program Budgeting.* Program Analysis and the Government. Cambridge: Harvard University Press, 1965.

Programs for Relocating Workers Used by Governments of Selected Countries. Paper No. 8 of Economic Policies and Practices. Prepared for the Joint Economic Committee of Congress. Washington: U.S. Government Printing Office, 1966.

Walter, Ingo. *The European Common Market, 1958–65.* Growth and Patterns of Trade and Production. New York: Frederick A. Praeger, Inc., 1966.

INDEX